T0062027

WITCH CRAFT

SIMPLIFIED

WITCHCRAFT SIMPLIFIED

13-Digit ISBN: 978-1-64643-252-3
10-Digit ISBN: 1-64643-252-5

This book may be ordered by mail from the publisher. Please include $5.99 for postage and handling. Please support your local bookseller first!

Books published by Cider Mill Press Book Publishers are available at special discounts for bulk purchases in the United States by corporations, institutions, and other organizations. For more information, please contact the publisher.

Cider Mill Press Book Publishers
"Where good books are ready for press"
PO Box 454
12 Spring Street
Kennebunkport, Maine 04046

Visit us online!
cidermillpress.com

Typography: Pandora Ep2, Sweet Sans Pro

Printed in China

All vectors used under official license from Shutterstock.com.

1 2 3 4 5 6 7 8 9 0
First Edition

WITCH CRAFT

SIMPLIFIED

SPELLS, MEDITATIONS & PRACTICES FOR THE MODERN WITCH

ISABELLA FERRARI

CIDER MILL
PRESS

BOOK
PUBLISHERS
KENNEBUNKPORT, MAINE

CONTENTS

CHAPTER 1
AN INTRODUCTION TO
WITCHCRAFT
6

CHAPTER 2
FIND YOUR OWN MAGICK
14

CHAPTER 3
THE POWER OF SEASONS
46

CHAPTER 4
SACRED SPACES AND TOOLS
60

CHAPTER 5
MAGICK AND CRAFTING
78

CHAPTER 6
CRAFTING IN YOUR KITCHEN
92

CHAPTER 7
SPELLS AND CHARMS
112

CHAPTER 1

AN INTRODUCTION
TO WITCHCRAFT

As human beings, we all need to find balance in our lives and fill our daily routines with good energy and positivity.

No matter your lifestyle or goals, there is no better way to explore the infinite number of ways to enjoy life than through Witchcraft. Through Witchcraft, we can learn to improve our lives and get in touch with our true selves by making use of all the tools that nature offers us.

Witchcraft has many different facets: you might follow the Wiccan path; you may be more interested in Traditional Witchcraft, Witchcraft based in Folklore, or Witchcraft based in magick and the land; or you might identify as a Green Witch, an Eclectic Witch, and so on.

The beauty of Witchcraft is that it is for everyone. It doesn't matter if you identify with other religions, if you are an atheist, or if you'd rather not label yourself and just want to learn some helpful practices.

The magick of the practices we will discover in the following pages, the incredible power of the seasons and the Wheel of the Year, and the spells and small rituals you can perform every day are the perfect path toward creating positive change in your life.

This is important: you don't have to identify as a Witch to practice Witchcraft.

There is a myth that you must be completely involved in the formal tradition, be part of a coven, or perform rituals every day to truly practice Witchcraft.

In truth, you are entitled to follow any aspects of Witchcraft that suit you; you choose your own path. This book will help you define your individual practice as you discover what works best for you.

Harmony, balance, positivity, and healing are the fundamentals of a good Witchy routine, which includes three essential aspects: yourself, your community, and the planet Earth.

Bringing magick to our lives is an act of self-love, and only by nourishing our mind and soul can we take care of the people around us.

Through spells and rituals, we will also learn about the natural magick that planet Earth offers us as we cohabitate with many types of animals, plants, and people. Discovering the energy and magickal properties of each individual will turn your own practice into one of balance, love, gratitude, and happiness.

Because we can create magick and improve our lives with what surrounds us (the typical herbs of the land, natural gifts we find during a walk in a park, seasonal fruit and vegetables, and so on), you don't have to spend a fortune to practice Witchcraft.

Although we might be highly influenced by the Witchy aesthetic that we see on social media, spending a large sum of money is not required to create something positive and magickal.

Everything we need is already around us. This book will help you find magick in your life—because everyone deserves to have it.

A BRIEF EXPLANATION OF PAGANISM AND WITCHCRAFT

The term "Pagan" comes from the Latin *paganus,* which means "rustic or rural," and it's used as an umbrella term that includes different philosophies, beliefs, and practices. However, everyone in the Pagan religion has a deep love and respect for nature and people.

Each individual or group might worship different gods and goddesses, perform different rituals, and celebrate different festivities. That all depends on their folklore and the land they live in.

Under the Pagan umbrella, we can find many varying branches such as Druidry, Shamanism, Asatru, Wicca, and so on. The last example is one of the most popular forms of Witchcraft nowadays, and the one that you will probably hear about in many situations connected to spirituality.

Wiccan people are very devoted to nature and the planet Earth. The Moon is their goddess and the Sun is their god. Although Wiccan Witches practice Witchcraft and are to be considered Pagan, the main characteristic of the Wiccan path is the

Rede—a statement of key morals, the fundamental beliefs of a system—that is at the base of their practice. The Wiccan Rede simply says *"An ye harm none, do what ye will."* That essentially means "do as you wish, as long as it doesn't harm anyone."

On the other hand, we can consider Witchcraft less of a religion and more of a practice that uses spellwork and magick (magick with a "k" differentiates the folk practice from that of a magician).

Witches or those who practice Witchcraft don't follow a specific set of rules; they are in charge of their ethics and morals. A Witch can have many practices and beliefs—this is where we get many of the different kinds of Witches.

Therefore, it is correct to say that all Wiccans are Witches and Pagans, but not all Pagans and Witches are Wiccans.

DIFFERENT KINDS OF MAGICK AND ETHICS

Magick and spellcraft are the arts of manipulating energies and influencing events with the intent of achieving what we desire.

To practice magick we need creativity, intuition, and knowledge, which is the most important element. That's why the word "Witch" means "wise woman," and why the word feels highly connected with something ancient and vast.

As mentioned in the introduction, there are many kinds of Witches. You might wonder: how will you find your path? The only way to find out is to get your hands dirty and try different charms, spells, Witchy routines, and experience them all until your heart tells you what is made for you.

Despite the fact that each path is personal and unique, we can still distinguish between different ways to perform magick:

FOLK WITCHCRAFT: the old, traditional practice, rooted in folklore before the 20th Century.

NATURAL MAGICK: suggests the use of aromatic herbs, stones, natural elements, and candles. It follows the influences of the moon and the sun.

CEREMONIAL MAGICK: includes precise ceremonies and rituals, often with the use of magickal tools. It is usually seen in Witch covens.

BLACK MAGICK: performed to hurt others or manipulate their minds and actions.

Wiccans have a strictly negative view on black magick, as they consider it very dangerous. Many think that only black magick has the ability to manipulate other people's minds; however, even a simple love spell (to make someone fall in love with you) can be considered a magick manipulation. As Witchcraft doesn't always follow the Rede, it comes down to our personal ethics to decide what magick we want to perform and what we think should be avoided.

Before making any decisions regarding the magick realm, we should ask ourselves:

WHAT ARE THE POSSIBLE CONSEQUENCES?

DO I HAVE AN ALTERNATIVE TO GET THE SAME RESULT?

Your ethics and knowledge will prevent you from creating negative energies and will make your practice a safe place.

CHAPTER 2

FIND YOUR OWN
MAGICK

In this book we will focus on everyday practices; there are no sacred books, ceremonies, prayers, rules, or spaces you need to utilize unless you choose to use them yourself for your own happiness.

Every single day of our life is sacred and important, and that's the main reason why we endeavor to make our daily routine magickal and beneficial. Your journey to improve your experience and create magick on a daily basis is the most sacred thing there is.

With that being said, we can incorporate some magickal tools into our daily practice that can help us to increase the power of our rituals and channel our energy in the right direction. Always choose the ones that feel right to you—and if you feel you don't need any of them, that is totally fine and won't obstruct your rituals and spells.

CAULDRON
- A pot, used for magickal purposes, connected to the divine feminine.

INCENSE
- It releases its magical properties when it burns.

- It represents the four elements (page 71).

CANDLES

- Fire symbolizes transformation.
- You will use candles for spells, rituals, and meditation.

HERBS

- Use them for spells, rituals, oils, salves, and potions.

BESOM

- A specific kind of broom.
- Use it to wipe away negative energies and to protect your home.

It can be extremely confusing when you are a beginner Witch to know where to focus your energy and what the essential aspects of a Witch's journey are.

Now that you know the main tools that can help you to direct your energies and give you the ability to change different situations and emotions, we shall review the key points that should be taken into consideration before performing spells and rituals.

Although these principles might vary depending on each individual's purpose, we can group together the main ones:

MINDFULNESS: to be aware of how our mind works and be present in the moment

BALANCE: harmony with ourselves, our community, and nature

HAPPINESS: to be content with who we are and what surrounds us

LOVE: affection and respect for ourselves, for others, and for our planet

ABUNDANCE: an overflowing of spiritual results, love, happiness, and prosperity, within our lives and others'

PROTECTION: keeping us, our house, our community, and nature safe from harm

It is essential that we be in control of our minds, as they are the most important magickal tools we have.

Meditation techniques and contact with nature are the best ways to be present in the moment and to guide our intent.

By developing mindfulness, our lives will be open to love and happiness that will fulfill not only ourselves, but also all the people around us and nature as a whole.

In order to care for others, we have to avoid surrounding ourselves with worries, and it's only when we have an abundance of what we need that we can worry less. If you lack an abundance of love, peace, or money, asking for it won't make you greedy; instead, it will put you in a position to care for others around you.

Protection is one of the fundamental aspects of Witchcraft, as it is the practice of safeguarding someone or something important to you.

You might want to protect yourself from negative energies or events, protect someone from evil entities, or protect your home from any unwanted energies or people. We will dive into more protection spells in the pages ahead.

MAKE YOUR HOME A MAGICKAL SPACE

In the past, the house of a Witch was the place where all magick happened, a sacred place to Witches, where they were protected and free to perform their rituals.

Heart Witches and Green Witches most commonly base the majority of their craft at home, performing protection rituals and keeping in strict contact with nature. They abide by a simple, home-based folk routine.

Your home is your sacred place, where you should feel re-charged and relaxed. That's why it's important to have a clean and pleasant space. Here are some tips that will help you to make your home a magickal place, attract good energies, and perform your rituals as effectively as possible.

PICK THE RIGHT COLORS

The magick energy of colors is one of the most powerful in the magick realm, and it's really easy to incorporate it into your daily practice.

You can pick the right color based on what your intent is, and you can integrate it into any of these objects:

- Candles
- Tablecloths
- Clothes
- Pens or crayons
- Furniture or walls
- Crystals and stones

RED is associated with the signs Aries and Scorpio. Its day is Tuesday, and its god is Mars. It is the color of passion, desire, courage, and sexual vigor.

ORANGE is associated with the sun. It's mostly connected with ambition in the business world, success, and careers in general. It is also affiliated with material needs, egocentrism, and self-belief.

YELLOW is associated with the sun, like the color orange. It is connected to all mental activities, intellectuality, and memory. This color can be used for protection and to increase imagination and creativity.

GOLD is associated with a general god that symbolizes all the masculine divinities. Its related sign is Leo, and it represents wealth and prosperity.

SILVER is associated with a general goddess that symbolizes all the feminine divinities. Its related sign is Cancer, and it's connected to femininity, intuition, and psychic abilities.

PINK is associated with Venus, and its related day is Friday. Its related signs are Taurus and Libra. It's connected to romantic love for others and ourselves. It brings positive values, affections, and peace.

GREEN is associated with planet Earth, harmony, and fertility. Like the color gold, it symbolizes prosperity. Performing a money spell with a banknote of this color can be very efficient.

LIGHT BLUE is associated with Jupiter. Its related day is Thursday and its related signs are Sagittarius and Pisces. It's connected with spiritual and creative activities, calm, patience, healing, trust, and good sleep.

PURPLE is associated with Mercury. Its related day is Wednesday, and its related signs are Gemini and Virgo. It's the color of the third eye, which represents spirituality, mystical intuition, and clairvoyance. It brings security, ambition, and knowledge in occultism.

BROWN is associated with nature, animals, and forests. It's a neutral color and can be used to send back any bad energy.

BLACK is associated with Saturn. Its related day is Saturday, and its related signs are Capricorn and Aquarius. It's connected to protection from bad energies and hexes, negative moments, and the "obscure side." The "obscure side" or "dark side" of Saturn is connected to the dark side of the self, the part of our personality that we want to hide or deny. It contains all the aspects we try to repress.

WHITE is associated with all the colors. If you can't find a specific color, white is the perfect substitute. It represents the purest form of femininity, childhood, maternity, and sincerity.

GET RID OF WHAT YOU DON'T NEED

It's so easy to overflow our houses and personal spaces with objects, books, and souvenirs, and as time goes by, we forget everything we own. The first rule for a tidy and magickal house is this: if you don't use it, throw it out. The more free space we have, the more our minds will relax and feel balanced.

HAVE A SPECIFIC SPACE FOR YOUR MAGICK

The rooms in our houses can be messy and busy, filled with our kids' toys, clothes, work papers, and so on. Once we have decided what we can throw away, we can find a little space where we can perform our spells and place our magical tools. It doesn't have to be a big part of our house, nor does it have to drastically change any room; it can be a small table, a shelf, or a drawer.

CLEANSE REGULARLY

Cleansing is the art of maintaining positive energies and getting rid of negative energies that might be present in ourselves, our house, an object, or someone else. Cleansing everything is a good start to bringing peace to our space.

Subsequently, you might want to find the heart of your home. This is the room used most often by you and the people who live with you. It's the room that contains a big amount of energy and therefore might make us feel unbalanced and uncomfortable if that energy is off. Although the most common tool for cleansing a space is white sage, for many it can be considered culturally wrong and not sustainable. Fortunately, there are plenty more ways to get rid of negativity.

THE ART OF CLEANSING AND PURIFYING

Cleansing is a practice that can be done in many different ways. The common denominator in all good cleansings, however, is your intent.

Your intent plays a significant role in every Witchy aspect; it will help you to achieve good results and perform positive routines.

Intent is the strong desire and determination to gain or achieve whatever you established before a practice. You can say it in your mind or out loud— either way, your higher self is putting out your needs and intents, and they can be directed to the universe, a specific god or goddess, spirits, or whatever energy you're working with.

As it is difficult sometimes to focus and feel like you are deep into the practice, don't beat yourself up if it takes time to feel successful in your intent. Only with constant practice and exercise will you develop your intent. But without a doubt, you will eventually get good results, as the magick is already in you—just as you would water a plant to make it grow, the same will be done with the Witch that is in you.

Without further ado, let's discover the main methods for cleansing and purifying.

CLEANSE WITHOUT ANY TOOLS

One of the most efficient ways to cleanse an object or a place is by using our hands. The energy that our body can emanate is truly powerful and beneficial to our lives, so why not use it to keep negativity away?

You can fill an object with your energy and—depending on your intent—the object will be empowered and ready to be used as a tool to achieve your goals. For example, you might cleanse a cleaning product, one of your makeup tools, or the clothes you want to wear. The procedure is easy and simple.

1 Hold the object with both your hands.
2 Take a few deep breaths to clear your mind.
3 Imagine white light coming out of your hand directly into the object.
4 While you do so, think deeply about your intent and enjoy all the good feelings.

From this moment on, you will be in touch with the object's magickal power and your day will be filled with positive energy. You can empower any object you want with positivity, happiness, peace, prosperity, or love.

CLEANSE A PLACE WITH INCENSE

Burning incense is an efficacious method to clear

a place from negative energies. It doesn't require a lot of time and it fills a room with a pleasant, magickal scent.

There are many different types of incense made with different ingredients. We will pick specific ingredients based on their properties, which will match with our intent.

Every herb, root, flower, and plant has its own attributes (page 27). That's why nothing is done at random; every ingredient has to be picked carefully.

You can buy premade incense. In that case, make sure it is 100% natural and environmentally friendly. You can also make homemade incense. Here is a simple recipe:

1 TEASPOON
FRANKINCENSE RESIN

2 TEASPOONS DRIED
ORANGE PEEL

1 TEASPOON
DRAGON'S BLOOD
RESIN

½ TEASPOON DRIED
LAVENDER

1 TEASPOON DRIED
ROSEMARY

1 Gently grind the resins (using a mortar and pestle, if possible) if necessary, but be careful not to make them too tiny and sticky.

2 Gather all the ingredients in a small jar. Make sure they are blended and well mixed.

3 Hold the jar in your hands and perform the cleansing technique we learned before.

4   Seal the jar carefully and label it.

5   When you want to use the incense, light a charcoal tablet and let it get hot for a few minutes. Sprinkle a bit of the mixture on the charcoal, place it in the center of a room, and let the smoke cleanse the entire space.

PURIFY YOUR HOUSE WITH A BROOM

It is popular to see representations of Witches holding a broom—more specifically, a besom. However, it is not always explained how a broom is used as a magickal tool. It is not advised that you use a plastic or nylon broom. Instead, buy a real straw-bristle broom or make one yourself.

The broom can be hung vertically on a wall (normally at the entrance of the house or in the kitchen) to protect the family and house, or it can be used to purify a space. In this case, we will use it to clean our floors.

1   Hold a broom in your hands and stand in the middle of the room.

2   Take deep breaths to clear your mind.

3   Start sweeping with your broom, imagining you are clearing away all negativity.

4   Walk around the room counterclockwise, making spiral, counterclockwise movements with your broom.

5   Visualize that each movement of the broom is sweeping away the negative energies of that room.

CLEANSING HERBS

Herbal magick is often used by Green Witches. Each herb—including weeds, flowers, roots, trees, and medical herbs—has its own magickal properties. According to those properties, you can choose your herb depending on the result you'd like to obtain. The way you can use these herbs are many and varied: you can burn them, make teas (always check if they are edible), use them in foods, baths, and so on.

Here are a few herbs that you can use to cleanse your house, a space, or a person:

ANISE: purification, love, luck, psychic abilities

BASIL: purification, prosperity, love, trust, luck

BAY: purification, protection, wisdom, psychic abilities

CHAMOMILE: purification, healing, peace

CINNAMON: purification, love, success, healing, money

ELDERFLOWER: purification, beauty, divination, sleep, money

JUNIPER: purification, protection against illness, fertility

LEMON: purification, happiness, protection

OAK: purification, prosperity, health, luck, strength

SAGE: purification, longevity, protection, health

THYME: purification, divination, healing, good sleep, courage

VERBENA: purification, blessings, communications with spirits

CRYSTALS AND STONES

The word crystal comes from the Greek "krystallos," which means "clear ice." Clear ice is a crystal that comes from a process called crystallization, and it signifies a transition from chaos to perfection.

The difference between a crystal and a stone is that a crystal is a solid substance with a natural geometric form and a shiny color; a stone is composed of more than one mineral and it's smoother, rounder, and denser than a crystal. Crystals and stones are another great way not only to cleanse and purify but also to enact various practices, depending on the special characteristics of each crystal or stone.

Each individual crystal and stone possesses specific energy that can affect the surrounding environment. Some can help boost your mood, others protect you and your house from bad energies, and others soothe anxiety and fears. Connecting to a crystal and embracing the vibration it emanates is a wonderful way to connect with your higher self and the universe.

In order to benefit from the power of healing crystals, you have to consciously set your intentions. That's why it's important to determine our goals, dreams, and desires before we pick a crystal. By considering the outcome we'd like to achieve, it will be much easier to decide what crystal or stone is best for us.

DIFFERENT SHAPES

Crystals can have many unique shapes. This depends on how the atoms that form a crystal repeat. A crystal created from salt can form the shape of a cube, for instance.

In spirituality and Witchcraft, each shape has a specific attribute:

CUBE
USED FOR GROUNDING

SPHERE
SENDS ENERGIES IN ALL DIRECTIONS

FREEFORM SHAPE
EMANATES HIGH VIBRATIONS

HEART
SENDS LOVE

GENERATOR TOWER
RECHARGES OTHER CRYSTALS

PYRAMID
SENDS INTENTIONS INTO THE UNIVERSE

MEDITATION STONE
TRANSFERS ENERGIES

TOWER
AMPLIFIES INTENTIONS

HEALING WITH CRYSTALS

Our body radiates with constant vibrations, and these can change based on how we feel: sad, happy, angry, tired, and so on. Each crystal has a specific vibration that can help us heal different aspects of our mind, body, and life.

That's why if we want to bring more peace to our home, there are crystals that we can place in the main room. If we want to heal our heart chakra, we can put a specific crystal on our chest and meditate.

These are only a few examples; the variety of ways you can heal with crystals are enormous. Let's get to know some of them better.

ROSE QUARTZ

Known for being powerful when used in fertility and love spells, rose quartz can bring love, ward off negativity, and protect from nightmares, fear, and anger. Never leave it under the sun for too long, as the sunlight will fade it. Cleanse it with tea, sage smoke, or bury it in the earth for twelve to twenty-four hours and then rinse it several times with water or rose water. It's associated with the goddesses Venus and Aphrodite, the heart chakra, the element of water, and the signs Libra and Taurus.

CITRINE

Citrine is a perfect crystal to manifest joyful thoughts and a peaceful atmosphere. It can bring wealth and abundance. It is also used to cleanse other crystals. It is associated with the god Mercury, the solar plexus chakra, and the element of air.

AMETHYST

Amethyst helps with cleansing, purifying, and healing the mind, body, and soul. It also helps to balance emotions and prevent irrational fears. You can cleanse it by burying it under salt or placing it under the moonlight on the night of a Full Moon. Avoid leaving it under the sun as that will fade its beautiful color. Amethyst is associated with Dionysus, Diana, and Bacchus, and with the signs Pisces, Aquarius, and Aries.

LAPIS LAZULI

Lapis lazuli can be used to increase psychic awareness and intuition. It is also used to manifest spiritual love and infuse fidelity into a relationship. You can cleanse it with singing bowls, incense, or under the moonlight. It is associated with the gods Venus and Isis, the throat and crown chakras, the elements of air and water, and the signs Sagittarius and Capricorn.

AVENTURINE

One of the most common crystals used in money spells, aventurine can bring luck and prosperity. It is also used to heal, calm mood swings, relieve stress, and bring peace. You can cleanse it with salt and moonlight. It is associated with the god Mercury, the third eye and heart chakra, the element of air, and the signs Libra and Taurus.

CLEAR QUARTZ

Clear quartz boosts the immune system, gives creative insight, and balances emotions. It can also purify the aura and the soul, protect from negative energies, and induce prophetic dreams. Cleanse frequently under the sunlight, with smoke, or in salty water. It is associated with the Great Mother, the crown chakra, the elements of water and fire, and the signs Cancer and Leo.

BLACK TOURMALINE

Black tourmaline is commonly worn to help minimize negative thoughts and doubts. It can bring self-confidence, personal power, and rational thinking. It is also perfect for scrying (a method of divination also known as crystallomancy—see page 76). It is associated with the goddess Manat, the element of water, and the signs Leo and Libra.

THE MAGICK OF CELESTIAL BODIES AND THE MOON

One of the most ancient traditions, practiced since the dawn of time, is observing the celestial bodies in the sky and drawing superstitions and hidden messages from them. As many believe, the alignment and position of different planets can affect a newborn's personality, and not only that: planets can affect our everyday life and boost the power of our spells.

SUN

The sun is the celestial body that gives us light and life. Along with the moon, it was the first celestial form that was believed to have magick. It represents masculine divinity. Its energy can be authoritarian and sometimes despotic. Its magickal attributes are health, success, authority, money, wealth, and strength.

MERCURY

Mercury is the nearest planet to the sun. Its energies and help are very inconstant. When you work with it, try to balance its energies with the energies of a more stable planet. When Mercury is in retrograde—when an optical illusion makes the planet appear to be moving backwards—you will experience negative energies, as you will struggle to communicate and plan things. Mercury's day is Wednesday, and its magickal attributes are communication, travel, psychic abilities, memory, creativity, sarcasm, and writing.

VENUS

Venus is located between Mercury and our planet, and although it is the moon that mostly influences women, Venus is also highly connected with the female gender. That's why the sign for Venus looks the same as the one that indicates the female gender.

Its day is Friday, and its magickal attributes are harmony, luxury, art, sexuality, desire, peace, pleasure, possessiveness, versatility, and relationships.

MARS

Mars is the planet that follows planet Earth. It's associated with the male world and its mysterious aspects. Compared to the sun, Mars has a much more aggressive and virile vibe, as it is also the planet of the god of war. Its day is Tuesday, and its magickal attributes are impulsivity, spirit of enterprise, selfishness, desire, action, freedom, sport, loyalty, conflict, and war.

JUPITER

Jupiter is the biggest planet in the solar system; that's why the king of gods shares its name. Its energies, compared to Mars or the sun, are more cerebral and regal. The best moment to perform a spell for justice or other affairs is on Jupiter day, which is Thursday. Its magickal attributes are truth, wealth, justice, success, knowledge, responsibility, politics, and optimism.

SATURN

Saturn was originally considered to be the farthest planet from the sun; that's why it was the last one to be associated with magick. It has masculine energy and is related to the Latin god Saturn, guardian of the fireside. Its energy guarantees protection. Therefore, it's good for spells to protect your house from unwanted energies. Its day is Saturday, and its magickal attributes are tenacity, overcoming obstacles, isolation, reliability, self-discipline, patience, isolation, and frugality.

URANUS

Uranus has bizarre energy, as its axis is horizontal and it rotates on itself. In mythology, Uranus is Chronos's (Saturn's) father and Zeus's (Jupiter's) grandfather. It doesn't have a lot of influence on our daily life respective to other planets. As it is not taken into consideration in the count of days and hours of the planets—meaning that it is not associated with a particular day or hour—to invoke its energy you can use an herb or plant associated with it. Its magickal attributes are eccentric ideas, inventiveness, and intense changes.

NEPTUNE

Neptune takes its name from the god of the sea, and because of that it is connected to water. Although it has fewer qualities than the other planets, it still affects our lives. Its magickal attributes are dreams, visions, ideas, fantasy, art, healing, illusion, and alchemy.

THE MOON

The Moon is the celestial body that has the most powerful effect on our life and routine. It has power over tides, harvests, and even over our physiological functions. That's why it is highly important in the magickal arts. Each moon phase contains specific characteristics and energies. Timing our spells to the different phases can be an excellent way to add power and magick to our lives. When performing a spell, you can use the crystal selenite to boost the power of the moon.

In the past, each month had a specific name for each moon, depending on different traditions. Here are some of the names you might find for each month:

JANUARY: Wolf Moon

FEBRUARY: Snow Moon

MARCH: Worm Moon

APRIL: Pink Moon

MAY: Flower Moon

JUNE: Strawberry Moon

JULY: Buck Moon

AUGUST: Red Moon

SEPTEMBER: Harvest Moon

OCTOBER: Blood Moon

NOVEMBER: Beaver Moon

DECEMBER: Cold Moon

The moon's magickal attributes are psychic abilities, connection to women, feminine energies, purity, beauty, dreams, protection, intuition, connection to children and newborns, spirituality, emotions, memory, instinct, imagination, and reincarnation.

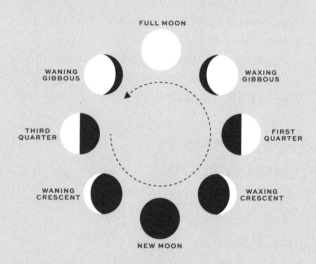

FULL MOON

WANING
GIBBOUS

WAXING
GIBBOUS

THIRD
QUARTER

FIRST
QUARTER

WANING
CRESCENT

WAXING
CRESCENT

NEW MOON

● NEW MOON

The New Moon is the first phase of the lunar cycle, when it is not visible in the sky, as the sun is behind it. This is the perfect time to start something and welcome new beginnings. It is advised you write down in your journal anything you would like to manifest in the upcoming month and meditate on your intentions.

It is also a perfect time to perform a full cleansing of your house and body. You can take a nice salt bath using Himalayan salt to cleanse your body from all stress and negative energies. To cleanse your house, you can use some white sage smoke or boil some water with a few rosemary branches. Once the water has cooled down, pour it in a spray bottle and spray the potion around your house, imagining all the bad energies disappearing immediately.

It is totally normal to feel unbalanced, tired, or particularly stressed during this time: listen to your body and mind and celebrate the chance to practice self-care. Resting your body, lighting a nice scented candle, or listening to some relaxing music might be everything you need to recharge your batteries.

● WAXING CRESCENT

The sun is now starting to move, and we can see the right side of the moon. The energies of the moon are slowly becoming more powerful at this time of the month, so you can focus on growth and all the new things that are entering your life. You can perform spells related to attraction, inspiration, and creation of new things.

If during the New Moon we set our goals and wrote down all the things we'd like to manifest, during the Waxing Crescent period, we should put our plans into action. With concrete actions and a good plan, we will be able to plant the seeds of our manifestations and see the first results.

We can meditate on self-belief and self-esteem to boost the confidence we have in ourselves and belief in what we want to do.

Though it's easy to get overwhelmed, try not to focus on more than one thing at a time. Remember that if we try to manifest too many things at once, our manifestation practice might become slow and inconsistent.

Visualize what you want to manifest, imagining all your goals as if you've already achieved them: enjoy the good feelings and the gratitude, and thank the universe. Do it every day in addition to journaling and meditating. Use this time to develop a positive mindset and focus on your goals.

◖ FIRST QUARTER

During the First Quarter, we are able to see the whole right side of the moon. While the first half of the moon is now lit and bright, the other one is still in the dark. It is a beautiful thing to see—the perfect balance between light and darkness—and inspires us to try and find the same balance in our life, a balance between desires and concrete plans, dreams and actions, visualization and manifestation.

This particular time of the month is accompanied by a significant increase of energies. If the New Moon was the time to set our goals, the First Quarter is the time to evaluate our actions, understand if we are on the right path, and determine if we can do more. Concrete steps are essential during this lunar phase. Take advantage of this energy boost to make difficult decisions and sort out problems.

If things aren't going as planned, take this time to reflect and understand what needs to be changed. You might feel like you're struggling, but remember that this time is all about commitment and tenacity. There is a solution for every problem; you just need to keep your focus on your goals. Change strategy if needed, and meditate on your self-belief and manifestation ambitions.

☽ WAXING GIBBOUS

During Waxing Gibbous, more than half of the moon is illuminated and only a small part is still in the dark. This is the last phase before the Full Moon, the moment where you need to push a little further in order to see the results. The energy of the moon is getting stronger and stronger, and you should feel how close you are to reaping what you sow.

Waxing Gibbous is the time to perform spells connected to success, realizations, and great achievements. There are only a few days before the Full Moon, the moment when you will see all the progress you've made. You can meditate on personal growth and your personal desires.

Not everything we want is ready to happen; we must put in all the effort we can and understand that we can't always get everything we want at the same time. Often patience and persistence are the keys to a good manifestation practice, and only experience will give us the tools to set the right goals at the right time.

Don't feel discouraged if you feel like you're far away from achieving all your goals; some plans require more time than others. The most important part of achieving your goals is the work you do after setting them. A quality manifestation practice is made of quality actions, even if sometimes it feels like we are behind. Those are all good things to meditate on during this lunar phase.

● FULL MOON

The Full Moon is considered the most important moment of the month for Witches, the time when we can admire the moon at its fullest beauty. The number of rituals and spells we can perform during this day is quite extensive: healing, protection, abundance, and guidance are the main aspects of this lunar phase.

The most common practice, though, belongs to the cleansing side of magick. You can cleanse your crystals by leaving them outside under the light of the Full Moon overnight and taking them back inside in the early morning. You might also want to make some "moon water" by pouring some water in a glass jar or bottle and leaving it outside your window or house. The water will absorb the power of the moon and afterwards you can drink it, use it for spells or potions, water your plants, or cleanse other tools.

After the moon reaches its fullest, it will slowly start fading its energies. You can use this moment to release anything unwanted: emotions, situations, people. It is normal to feel full of energy but, at the same time, emotionally drained. Always listen to your body and mind. If you feel tired, overwhelmed, in pain, or unbalanced, it is best to postpone your spell plans and rest your body. It is important to be at our best when performing spells as we work with a lot of energy and power. Listening to what our body and mind need is extremely important to ensure a healthy and efficient practice.

GROWING HERBS WITH THE MOON
The lunar phases are very important in agriculture.

Many Witches and non-practitioners use the moon cycle to grow their plants. The moon is not only related to magick arts: it has a strong influence over water and other liquids. If you're a Witch or you'd like to connect more with the moon, you can follow its cycle to try and grow some plants for your spells and rituals.

FROM THE NEW MOON TO THE FIRST QUARTER: Plant leafy greens and herbs.

FROM THE FIRST QUARTER TO THE FULL MOON: Plant flowers and above-ground vegetables.

FROM THE FULL MOON TO THE THIRD QUARTER: Plant root vegetables and bulbs.

FROM THE THIRD QUARTER TO THE NEW MOON: Plant weeds and maintain your other plants and vegetables.

By following these stages, you can also figure out what's best to use for your spells and how to create a perfect magickal garden. Also keep the life cycle of a plant in mind:

NEW MOON: seeds

CRESCENT MOON: sprouts

WAXING MOON: growth

FULL MOON: fruit/flower

WANING MOON: harvest

NEW MOON: preparation for new growths

As you grow your plants and herbs, note all the details and personal thoughts in your Book of Shadows. The Book of Shadows is a personal journal where a Witch can record everything that she has learned: spells, magickal definitions, and personal thoughts on her practice. By doing so you'll create a perfect guide on how to grow any plants and herbs.

CHAPTER 3

THE POWER OF SEASONS

The solar year is made of four different parts: the four seasons, which each have their own characteristics and therefore different kinds of impact on our lives. For a Witch, it is really important to observe the seasons changing and know what they will bring as they can impact our practice.

Sitting down on the first day of a season, looking around us and meditating on all the changes that are happening around us, is indeed a special moment to honor nature and feel connected to it. The amazing rhythm of nature brings us different smells, flavors, herbs, fruit, and vegetables, and so our rhythms change with it. Always be aware of the changing of the seasons, as it will impact your energy, environment, and practice.

The seasonal changes bring with themselves four different phases:

SPRING EQUINOX TO SUMMER SOLSTICE:
growing

SUMMER SOLSTICE TO AUTUMN EQUINOX:
harvesting

AUTUMN EQUINOX TO WINTER SOLSTICE:
resting

WINTER SOLSTICE TO SPRING EQUINOX:
cleansing

These four phases can be a mirror to different phases in your life.

The cycle can affect your career, relationships, and personal life.

Witches and Pagans are known for celebrating every solstice and equinox, following what's called the Wheel of the Year. Beyond the opportunity to feel connected with nature, these festivities can allow us to interact with our natural environment, which we can do by spending the day outdoors or walking through woods or parks (maybe picking up little decorations for our home or altar), always respecting nature.

With that said, there are no formal ways to celebrate the changing of the seasons. Every Witch creates her own way of expressing gratitude to nature and Earth. And that unique ritual will be part of her growth in heart, spirit, and mind.

THE WHEEL OF THE YEAR

In the Pagan culture, we can find—corresponding to the equinoxes and solstices—the eight Sabbats. The Sabbats are festivities to celebrate the changing of the seasons and what they bring to our life.

In the folklore, we find many communities and villages reunited, commonly around a fire or in the square, celebrating each festival at different times of the year.

The eight Sabbats form the Wheel of the Year, which groups the eight festivals and their dates and symbols. Every Sabbat brings with it different herbs, colors, spells, foods, and rituals.

It is important to know, however, that not every Witch celebrates the Sabbats; some only celebrate Samhain, others celebrate some of them, and other Witches celebrate none of them. There aren't specific rules to follow or obey; there aren't spells or rituals you must perform.

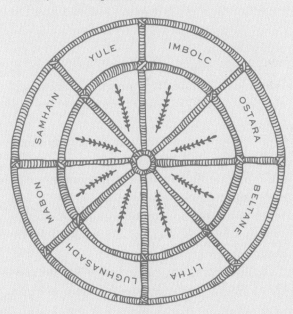

As the Sabbats help us to align with Mother Nature, you are free to find your own way to celebrate the seasons, discovering what you enjoy the most and what makes you feel more comfortable. The most important thing is to respect others and nature and figure out what is right for you.

SAMHAIN

Samhain, pronounced sow-een, falls between the autumn equinox and winter solstice, celebrated around the 31st of October and the 2nd of November. We might already be familiar with these dates as they're related to Halloween, el Día de los Muertos (the Day of the Dead), and All Saints Day.

The Celtic people used to live in what we now call Britain, Ireland, and Northern France. These days for them signaled the end of the year, as the harvest time was over and the cold winter was starting. Winter was a very lightless part of the year, associated with human death. That's why it was easy for spirits to enter the human realm. Some spirits were more than welcome. As for others, a good guard was required. Big bonfires were built in the center of town, where people met to dance around the fire and tell each other stories.

Today, Wiccans, Pagans, and other Witches celebrate Samhain in different ways. It is still a wonderful day to honor ancestry and spirits and welcome the start of a cold and dark part of the year.

SAMHAIN SYMBOLS

ANIMALS: black cat, owl, raven, bat

COLORS: orange, black, brown, gold, purple

FOOD: apples, gingerbread, soul cakes, cider, muffins, pumpkin

GODS AND GODDESSES: all Crone goddesses, all ancestors and spirits, Hecate, Persephone, Dionysus

HERBS: cinnamon, allspice, hazel, sage, nightshade

INCENSE: mint, sage, apple, nutmeg

STONES: carnelian, onyx, smoky quartz, bloodstone

SYMBOLS: jack-o'-lanterns, pumpkins, cauldrons, balefire

YULE

Yule is celebrated during the Winter solstice, originating in a Germanic tradition. As many already know, the majority of present-day Christmas traditions were taken from Yule. People celebrated a turning point—the promise that winter will be over.

Many families gather together, exchanging food and stories; other traditions involve the singing of songs and visiting friends and neighbors. Different types of food, alcoholic beverages, and gifts might be given by or brought to visitors.

The energy of the winter solstice supports the magick related to turning points, new beginnings, family relationships, world peace, and renewals. It is advised that you perform sun-related spells at sunrise during this time.

YULE SYMBOLS

ANIMALS: bear, eagle, deer, squirrel, sow, goose

COLORS: red, green, white, gold, silver, blue

FOOD: potatoes, apples, nuts, highly spiced bread, cakes, alcoholic beverages

GODS AND GODDESSES: Diana, Freya, Apollo, Cronos, Green Man, Holly King, Thrym

HERBS: blessed thistle, chamomile, peppermint, rosemary, sage

INCENSE: cedar, frankincense, cinnamon, pine

STONES: clear quartz, bloodstone, emerald

SYMBOLS: bells, candles, Yule log, snowflakes, goddess figure

IMBOLC

Imbolc is considered a late-winter, early-spring festival, celebrated around the 1st and the 2nd of February. Despite the presence of a still strong winter, there are some signs of spring and the cattle begin to give birth.

As it is another Celtic fire festival, fires must be re-lit, using Yule greenery. The bonfire is also an invitation for faeries to stay in the house; candles are placed on windows to welcome spring, and house purification rituals are performed.

A fun tradition in the early days of this holiday was when people would go around the village making noise with pans and pots. Every family used to welcome the group and offer them food and drinks. Groups would decorate a plow and kids went house-to-house to ask for treats; if the house owner declined, the front yard was plowed up.

IMBOLC SYMBOLS

ANIMALS: cow, lark, snake, sheep

COLORS: white, pink, yellow, red, brown

FOOD: dairy products, spicy food, lamb, smoked meat, dried fruit, nuts

GODS AND GODDESSES: Brigid, Persephone, Vesta

HERBS: angelica, basil, bay, holly, violets, thyme

INCENSE: basil, bay, cinnamon, vanilla, violet

STONES: bloodstone, ruby, onyx, amethyst

SYMBOLS: besoms, white flowers, Brigid's cross, corn dolly

OSTARA

Ostara takes place at the time of spring equinox. It represents the time of new growth and the fertility of the earth. The name comes from the goddess Ostara/Eostre, and she symbolizes rebirth, growth, and renewal.

Similar to Easter, symbols associated with Ostara include eggs, seeds, and rabbits. To celebrate, you can decorate your house or altar with fresh flowers and plants. Like Imbolc, this time of year is perfect to clean and purify your house and yourself. Meditate on your old habits and ask yourself if you're ready to let go of all the things that don't make you happy.

It is also the right moment to plant the seeds of whatever you'd like to manifest in the coming months: literally, if you have a garden, and figuratively, in terms of spellwork.

OSTARA SYMBOLS

ANIMALS: bee, butterfly, rabbit, hedgehog, horse, robin

COLORS: bright green, purple, yellow

FOOD: hot cross bun, Vernal Equinox cake, eggs, honey, milk, herbal teas

GODS AND GODDESSES: Aphrodite, Bel, Horned God, Diana, Thor

HERBS: ash, basil, bay leaves, cherry blossom, daffodil, dandelion, primroses

INCENSE: rose, jasmine, lavender, myrrh

STONES: aquamarine, lapis lazuli, agate

SYMBOLS: spring flowers, bunnies, colorful eggs, butterflies

BELTANE

Beltane is a spring festival celebrated around April 30th and May 1st.

It is considered almost the opposite of Samhain. As some say, the faeries won't hide from the cold anymore and they can return, bringing a magickal atmosphere with them.

The Maypole is a traditional Beltane dance, where the pole represents the male and the ribbons the female. People filled a basket full of goodies and instead of asking for gifts—as in Samhain—they hung the basket on their friend's doorknob.

Beltane is another fire festival of the Wheel of the Year. Many sacrifices were performed around the fire; although this is not acceptable in modern society, we can use the fire as a ritual fumigation.

BELTANE SYMBOLS

ANIMALS: chick, butterfly, bee, pooka

COLORS: green, blue, pink, yellow

FOOD: dairy, cherry, strawberry, salad, May wine

GODS AND GODDESSES: Bel, Belenos, Apollo, Bacchus, Cupid, Eros, Frey

HERBS: honeysuckle, hawthorn, rose, lilac, all flowers

INCENSE: frankincense, rose, musk, ylang-ylang

STONES: rose quartz, garnet

SYMBOLS: wreaths of flowers, Maypole, ribbons, cauldron, strings of beads

LITHA

Litha is a summer solstice festivity, celebrated around the 21st of June. The name comes from the Anglo-Saxon word "Līþa" and means "mid-summer." During this time, the power of the sun starts easing; the days get shorter and the nights get longer, and we embrace the dark to complete the Wheel of the Year.

Traditionally, people stayed awake all night on Midsummer's Eve to watch the sunrise. Bonfires made with oak wood were lit on the top of sacred hills, and aromatic herbs were thrown in. This ritual represented the strength of the sun and honored it.

People danced around the fire and blessed animals with the blazing herbs.

LITHA SYMBOLS

ANIMALS: cattle, horse, snake, sea creatures

COLORS: The natural world is full of colors at this time, so you can pick your favorite one!

FOOD: herbed bread, pastries, red wine, vegetables, cheese, cold cooked meat

GODS AND GODDESSES: Anu, Aphrodite, Juno, Apollo, Jupiter

HERBS: cinquefoil, chamomile, lavender, thyme, mugwort

INCENSE: orange, cinnamon, frankincense

STONES: amber, jade, moonstone, tiger's eye

SYMBOLS: solar cross, flowers, fruits, seashells

LUGHNASADH

Lughnasadh is a harvest festival celebrated on the 1st of August. Traditionally, competitions of skills and strength were performed, and as with many other festivals, there were bonfire dances. Fields and cattle were blessed with the ash from the bonfire, a wonderful feast took place, and all the participants consumed part of the gods' offering.

When it rains on this day, it is a blessing from

the god Lugh. It is a tradition to save the water for future rituals. This festival was and remains a special day for handfasting and weddings.

In the modern day, people who celebrate Lughnasadh gather together to celebrate the sun and the harvest deities, enjoying the day with their community.

LUGHNASADH SYMBOLS

ANIMALS: crow, calf, pig, rooster, salmon

COLORS: golden, yellow, green

FOOD: bread in the shape of humans or gods, blackberries, blueberries

GODS AND GODDESSES: Lugh, Tailtiu, harvest deities

HERBS: wheat, oak leaves, myrtle, acacia flowers

INCENSE: sandalwood, frankincense

STONES: amber, aventurine, citrine, clear quartz, obsidian

SYMBOLS: grains, berries, agricultural tools, sunflowers, sun wheels

MABON

Mabon is a harvest festival celebrated at the autumn equinox. The name was assigned in the 1970s by Aiden Kelly, but no historical proof was found that confirms the use of this name by ancient populations.

During this time people celebrate the balance of light and dark, life and death, and other opposing forces, with the understanding that darkness will reign in the upcoming months until Ostara.

It is also celebrated as a thanksgiving day, where Witches and others who celebrate gather their symbolic (or not) harvest and thank the gods for their help and other spirits and ancestors. This day is celebrated by eating good food, drinking, and sharing a general sense of gratitude.

MABON SYMBOLS

ANIMALS: blackbird, owl, eagle, wild goose, wolf

COLORS: red, brown, cream, gold, purple

FOOD: dried fruits, squash, pies, apples, beans, chicken, wine

GODS AND GODDESSES: Bona Dea, Demeter, Bacchus, Dionysus, Hermes

HERBS: chamomile, yarrow, marigold, bittersweet

INCENSE: pine, clove, cinnamon, apple, sage

STONES: cat's eye, clear quartz, aventurine, amber, sapphire

SYMBOLS: pumpkin, dried corn, autumn leaves, flowers, animals' image

CHAPTER 4

SACRED SPACES AND TOOLS

A Witch's magickal practice can include sacred objects that will assist her in spells and rituals. Sacred tools are not required for your practice; the most important and powerful things are your mind and voice. However, if you decide to incorporate other objects, it is better to buy them without rushing. Allow yourself to find the right ones for you; this will certainly require some time.

If you're not an experienced practitioner, it might be difficult sometimes to focus and visualize your energy during a spell or a ritual, and tools can aid in this. Moreover, the use of the tools helps us to distance ourselves from mundane reality and get into the magick realm more quickly and easily. It is far more efficient, at times, to visualize our energy coming out the end of a dagger instead of the end of our finger.

However, no matter what we use, if we are focused and able to lead our energy in the right direction, the outcome of a spell will be the same. We should see our tools as an additional help to channel our energies and intentions.

The most common tools are:

- Wand
- Chalice
- Athame (dagger)
- Cauldron
- Broom

All of these tools and others can be kept on an altar; although even the altar is not essential. There is also a specific uniform that some Witches wear to perform their magick. A sacred vest has to be long, with a hood and no sleeves (or sleeves that stay tight to the wrists). The color will depend on the seasons: light (in color and weight) material for spring and summer, and dark and heavy material for autumn and winter.

TOOLS AND THEIR USES

WAND

The wand is one of the most important tools for a Witch. It is associated with the element of air, but some Witches associate it with the element of fire as well.

A wand will help you channel your energy and direct it to a specific object or person, and to open or close a magick circle. Some Witches use a big stick instead of a wand, while some use both. Typically, a wand is made of wood; this can be from an oak, willow, ash, holly, maple, or apple tree.

The length of a wand can vary, but it is normally as long as the distance between your finger and your elbow. It has to be narrow, without knots, and polished. Once you have your wand, you can keep it clean and simple or decorate it with feathers, strings, colorful leather, or crystals.

CHALICE

The chalice is associated with feminine energy, the element of water, and fertility. It is used to contain the offer of a drink during a ceremony or ritual. Some Witches use a cup or a jug.

A chalice must be quite resistant so it won't break in case it's dropped.

It can be made of terracotta, wood, stone, or metal (silver, gold, bronze). It is also important to not use cups from our kitchen: sacred tools must be used only during magickal practices.

ATHAME

The athame, along with the wand, is the most important tool for a Witch. It is associated with the element of fire, and some Witches associate it with the element of air as well. Its blade can be made of metal, iron, stone, or crystal, and it can be straight or wavy. Its handle can be made of wood or stone. The length is normally around 15 cm.

The athame is generally used during rituals, to open and close magick circles, channel energy, and invoke deities. If you work with faeries you shouldn't get an iron or metal sword; avoid plastic daggers as well.

CAULDRON

A cauldron is commonly made of iron. Although we often see it in movies with Witches, it is not fundamental, as we could use a normal pot in its place. However, it can be helpful. It is considered a source of wisdom and nourishment, associated with the elements of water and fire.

Witches can use it in any spells, especially the ones connected to transformation: to burn herbs, papers, and other items used in spells, to make potions, and during the Sabbats. It is very important to keep your cauldron clean and to purify it after an intense spell or if you lend it to another Witch. As mentioned before, it is advised you use your cauldron only for magick purposes and keep it away from your kitchen and other normal pots.

BROOM

The broom—also known as the besom—is another important tool in a Witch's trousseau. The dimension is not important; even a small one can do. The handle can be made of birch, hazelnut, oak, or ash wood. The bristles can be made of straw, twigs, lavender, mugwort, or thyme.

Its use is to purify or to protect if hung next to a front door. If you can't build your broom and you have to buy it instead, try to avoid brooms in supermarkets with glue and plastic parts and those that are made for domestic use. You can find a proper magick broom in any esoteric shop.

SECONDARY TOOLS

Beyond the most common tools, a Witch can incorporate other tools into her collection. Again, don't feel like you have to buy any or all of them.

As time passes you will become more experienced, and you'll learn which tools help your practice and which don't. Secondary tools include:

A PENTACLE

The pentacle can be made of terracotta, metal, wood, or simply drawn on a piece of paper. Many Wiccans traditionally wore the pentacle as a jewel. It is also placed on magickal objects during spells— like candles, incense, or crystals—to increase the energy. The tips of the pentacle indicate the five different elements: water, fire, earth, air, and spirit.

It can be used as is or upside down; it doesn't have any negative connotation or link to black magick.

A BELL

When a Witch closes a magick circle, she can ring a bell to announce and signify her entrance to another dimension. At the end of a ritual, when she opens the magick circle, she can ring the bell again to come back to the normal world. A bell can also be used to send away negative spirits: you can either ring it or hang seven bells outside your front door.

PARCHMENT

Traditionally, spells are written on parchment papers. In ancient times, this paper was made from sheep's skin. Today we can find many types of parchment that do not come from animals' skin. In the course of various spells, it is required you burn pieces of parchment with parts of the spell written on it. Pay close attention, as parchment burns very quickly; in fact, you could use a cauldron to let the paper burn.

ALTARS

Altars are a sacred space where a Witch can practice her magick. They can be dedicated to deities, spirits, people, or to a particular aspect of life. An altar can be permanent or temporary.

No matter what type of altar you'd like to have, it is very important to take care of it, keep it clean, and respect it. You can have an indoor altar or an outdoor one. In the first case, you can create it on a shelf in your house, on a small desk, on a chair, or even in a box or jar if you want to keep it private. If you'd like to perform your magick outdoors, you can find a place in your garden. However, it is best to avoid leaving objects that can be ruined by water or put animals at risk (small crystals, sweet food, or a dagger). It is important to always place your altar in a space where it won't be disturbed or broken by anyone.

Traditionally, an altar for rituals should be placed facing north. However, you can place it wherever it feels more comfortable for you.

Every altar is decorated with a table cloth. If the altar is permanent, you can use one table cloth and pick the color you like the most; if the altar is temporary, the color should match its purpose.

The items on your altar are very personal. You can choose to include pictures, flowers, candles, crystals, pieces from nature, and so on.

There's a traditional way to set an altar for rituals. You don't have to follow this set, but it might be helpful in case you need a reference.

Each element represents a force of nature and is associated with a cardinal point:

NORTH: associated with the earth—we can place a stone

EAST: associated with air—we can place our wand

WEST: associated with water—we can place a chalice

SOUTH: associated with fire—we can place an athame

The green candle represents the Goddess and the red the God.

In the center we place the candle we will use for our spell, while we place a pentacle and the other ingredients for the spell near to us.

BLESSING AN ALTAR

Altars need to be purified, especially if they're permanent altars, as they can hold negative energies. We learned how to purify a space or object in Chapter 2 (page 22), and we can pick the purifying method we most like to make sure our altar is clean from any unwanted energies. Here is a purifying method that might help you to purify your permanent altar:

1 Light some white sage and purify the space with the smoke.

2 Create a magick circle (page 70) and invoke the elements, saying:

> AIR, ELEMENT OF EAST
>
> FIRE, ELEMENT OF SOUTH
>
> EARTH, ELEMENT OF NORTH
>
> WATER, ELEMENT OF WEST
>
> I INVOKE YOU, MY GUARDIANS,
>
> JOIN ME
>
> AND BLESS MY ALTAR,
>
> HAIL AND WELCOME TO MY CIRCLE.

3 Light a white candle and put it in the center of your altar. Close your eyes and imagine a white light surrounding your altar.

4 When the ritual is over, open your eyes and say, "This altar is now blessed."

5 Set the elements free and open your circle.

A MAGICK CIRCLE

Every spell should be performed inside a magick circle.

A magick circle is a consecrated space that you create using your finger, wand, or athame. It has three main functions: it separates you from the mundane world, it contains magickal energies until you're ready to let them go, and it protects you from all the negative energies outside the circle.

Some Witches prefer to draw a circle with salt or chalk and position a candle for each element on top of it. You can use whatever method works best for you.

Technically, when you create a circle, it is called "closing a circle." When you are finished and you need to break the circle, it is called "opening a circle."

To close a circle, you'll need to:

1 Position yourself toward north (if that's not possible because your altar is near the wall, you can stand in front of it).
2 Point your finger of your dominant hand, a wand, or an athame toward the floor in front of you.
3 Walk clockwise, imagining a sphere of energy around you.

4 While walking, say: "I close this sacred circle. I now am between the two worlds."

5 Invoke the elements and perform your spell.

To invoke the elements, position yourself toward north, and point your finger or sacred tool upward. Each cardinal point corresponds to an element, so for the invocation of each element walk in the corresponding cardinal point:

- North is Earth, the symbol of wisdom and strength.

- East is Air, the symbol of inspiration and mind.

- West is Water, the symbol of intuition and emotions.

- South is Fire, the symbol of passion and energy.

The invocation prayer for the four elements is:

"I INVOKE THEE, SPIRIT OF [CARDINAL POINT]

PLEASE, JOIN ME NOW AND GRANT ME THE POWER OF [THE ELEMENT]

BLESSED BE!"

Once you've closed your circle and invoked the elements, you can perform your ritual or spell of choice. Remember that if your spell includes the invocation of a deity, you should do it after the invocation of the four elements, once the circle is closed. At the end of your spell or ritual, you'll have to set free the element and open your circle.

To set free the four elements, go back to where you started when you invoked them. Facing outward, point your finger of your non-dominant hand, wand, or athame upward and say:

"SPIRIT OF [CARDINAL POINT]
THANK YOU FOR JOINING ME AND
GIVING ME THE POWER OF [THE ELEMENT].
STAY IF YOU WILL, GO IF YOU MUST.
I SET YOU FREE!"

Once this is done, the last thing left to do is to open your circle. As you did to set free the four elements, go back to where you started when you closed your circle. Then, you'll have to walk counterclockwise. You will absorb the energy of the circle with your non-dominant hand through your finger, wand, or athame. While walking, say:

"THIS CIRCLE IS NOW OPEN BUT NOT BROKEN.
WITH HARM TO NONE,
AS THE MAGICKAL CANDLES
CEREMONIOUSLY GLOW,
THIS CIRCLE MUST NOW END
SO MOTE IT BE!"

Now all the energies or entities within are banished; if you have drawn your circle with salt or chalk, you can now clean it. The energetic barriers are removed and your space is back to normal.

DIVINATION

Divination is the art of foreseeing the future, past events, and unknown and hidden aspects of our reality. By doing so we are able to find the answers to various questions regarding our existence and personal matters.

Most Witches know how to perform at least one type of divination. You can practice it by using tools or by using the power of your mind. It can be done by using tarot cards, for example, or by contacting spirits, although that practice is accessible only to a few.

When we want to perform any divination practice, we must be sure to have a clear mind and be confident in what we are doing. You can obtain a clear and focused mind by meditating every day, focusing on mindfulness. You can sit down on a comfortable seat and light a candle, close your eyes, and let all the thoughts float from your mind and slowly disappear.

If you get distracted, count to three and start again. You will be ready to start when your mind can stay clear and away from all the intrusive thoughts that could distract you from your divination ritual. It is highly advised that you keep notes on all your progress, thoughts, and experiences in your Book of Shadows (page 45). This way you will be able to track everything you learn and eventually record some important answers that you'll discern from the rituals.

TAROT CARDS

Tarot cards are the most common tool for divination. They are not made to read the future, exactly, but to gain a clearer vision regarding personal situations.

The deck is made of seventy-eight cards, divided into twenty-two Major Arcana and fifty-six Minor Arcana. The word "Arcana" means "secrets." The Major Arcana represent lessons that affect your life, soul, and long-term experiences. The Minor Arcana represent the day-to-day and mundane aspects of your life. Each card has a specific meaning, and a combination of two or more cards can indicate something specific to be taken into consideration.

There are many types of decks with different graphic representations. It is crucial you find the right deck for you, without rushing the process. Before purchasing a deck, study the cards: try and hold them and see how you feel. Many Witches own more than one deck, and each of them is used for specific situations.

When you're not using the cards, take good care of them; always put them in their box or in a cloth bag. It is customary to wrap them in a black cloth to protect them from negative energies. If the deck is giving you problems, you can cleanse them using the various methods explained in previous chapters (page 22).

RUNES

Runes are symbols that originate from the Norse tradition, usually painted or carved on stones or wooden disks. Modern runes are made of twenty-four symbols divided into three groups of eight: the first is associated with the deities Frey and Freya, the second is associated with Heimdall, and the third is associated with Tyr. Sometimes you might find an empty rune that symbolizes fate, but it was not part of the original tradition—so it is up to you whether you want to use it or not.

They have to be placed in a specific order, and their combination gives us the answer to whatever question we ask. You can find them in esoteric shops or you can decide to make them yourself.

The process of making them is not too difficult. Find little stones or wooden disks, and then you can decide to paint each symbol or carve it into your stone or disk; any method is fine as long as the symbols are clear and readable. Once the runes are made, purify them and keep them in a silk or velvet bag.

CRYSTALLOMANCY (OR "SCRYING")

You've probably seen one of the many depictions of a Witch or a psychic using a crystal ball to see future scenes. That is part of what crystallomancy is: a technique that doesn't require the knowledge of complex symbols. However, it is one of the most difficult practices, as it relies on the power of the mind.

It is important to state that the messages we receive through crystallomancy are not a product of our mind but come from deities or spirits, depending on whom we work with. The best herbs to burn before practicing crystallomancy are:

- Rosemary
- Sage
- Thyme
- Mugwort
- Parsley

The main tools we can use to practice crystallomancy are these three:

CRYSTAL BALL: In a dark room, light a candle and look into the crystal ball. You won't be able to see images inside the ball, but rather in your mind. Take note and analyze what you saw.

MIRROR: It has to be black and be placed on a horizontal surface. You can place one candle in the middle of it, or two candles by the sides. When you look in the mirror, you will see images in your mind.

SMOKE: It can come from incense or a candle. You will see shapes or symbols in the smoke. Pay attention to them and determine your interpretation using what you see.

These are only some of the methods you can use if you'd like to learn how to practice divination. Some Witches use the surface of water to look for answers; others perform automatic writings through the help of spirits. Whatever you pick, always start this practice with a clear and peaceful mind.

It is not advised that you attempt this sort of practice after an argument with someone, a stressful day, or when energies are very low. Never force your perception—let the answers come to you naturally. Take note of what you see without wasting too much time writing down every detail or you might lose focus. When visions end, you can take all the time you need to understand your notes and determine your interpretations.

CHAPTER 5

MAGICK AND CRAFTING

In this chapter, we will be talking about the many different ways we can create magick with our hands by crafting and spending time in our kitchen. All the crafts will be plant- and herb-based. It is important to always know the magickal and medicinal attributes of what we use.

Be careful of the potential allergies you might have and all the side effects of what you choose to work with. For example, when burning some herbs, the smoke can be dangerous to inhale or hallucinogenic; other herbs might contain poison or be good only for external use. You can write in your Book of Shadows (page 45) all the magickal attributes of each plant you use, in addition to adding labels to your jars with the dates and the ingredients.

If you chose to implement mostly herbs in your craft, it is best to learn how to store them and harvest them while respecting the environment and the vegetation. When you go to your garden to harvest your herbs, take note of what you need to use, whether it's the leaves, the roots, or the flowers. Never rip a whole plant out of the ground. Doing that will damage the roots and the plant won't be able to keep growing. Take from a plant only what you need and make sure to avoid damaging it. A lot of Witches, with respect to their plants, are used to asking permission from each plant before taking its leaves and flowers, and thanking them once the work is done.

If you're using fresh herbs, it is advised that you use them as soon as you pick them; if you want to store them, then they have to be fully dried for good conservation. To dry fresh plants, you can leave them laying down on an old cloth or surface in a well-ventilated area.

If you want to dry plants with their full stems, you can tie them with an elastic or rope and hang them upside down by fastening them to a spike or hanging herbs. The area has to be dry and ventilated—if you can hang them in a dark space like a closet, that's even better. It is helpful to attach a small label with the name of the plant to each so you don't forget it.

If you don't have time to wait until the plants dry, you can take their leaves and flowers and warm them in the oven. The temperature has to be around 100–110°F and the door has to be slightly open. Keep checking to make sure you don't burn them, and once they are ready, store them in an air-tight jar.

After completing whatever procedure you chose, thank the plant, and if you have some time, spend it meditating on gratitude and love for nature and Mother Earth.

DRINKING MAGICK HERBS

Extracting the properties and magickal attributes of a plant is one of the simplest ways to benefit from it. Boiling some water with a plant of choice is certainly one of the first methods a beginner Witch could learn and try. However, there are several different ways to extract the properties and magickal attributes of plants that we should know about. Then, we can choose the appropriate method for different situations, depending on the outcome we'd like to achieve. The main ones are:

DECOCTION: This method includes the boiling of water, usually around one to four liters, along with the plant of choice for about two hours. It's a strong extraction method used mostly for stems, roots, rhizomes, and bark.

INFUSION: In this process, we first boil the water (or other liquids), and then pour it over the herbs for a period of time, collecting the water, and strain them at the end. With an infusion, we can make teas, oils, salves, flavored waters, etc.

MACERATION: This process turns our herbs into a solvent, like alcohol or vinegar, for example. The final liquid is called a "tincture," a term usually used for medicinal purposes. You can add a few drops in water or some honey to then be consumed.

OTHER HERBAL CRAFTS

Now that we have discussed some of the main methods for working with liquids and herbs, we can move on to another combination of ingredients—a liquid and another base. Examples of this include:

SOAPS: Take your herbal extract liquid and mix with your base to make soap (the base can be lye, Marseille soap, or a base of fat with the functionality of a soap bar). You can add some essential oils if you'd like to. To decorate it, once you pour it into a mold, add dry flowers. Magickal soaps clean your body not only of dirt but also negative energies.

SALVES: Get some beeswax and melt it by putting a small jar in a pan with water on low heat. Add the liquid (herbal oils made with olive oil, coconut oil, etc.). You can also add some essential oils if needed. Let it cool down and use it by rubbing it into your body or an object.

DIFFERENT TYPES OF SALVES

Salves are very potent and beneficial to our body and spirit. Depending on what essential oil you add, they can be used as perfumes as well. As they melt when rubbed onto our skin, they can get rid of pains, irritations, and also bring us positive emotions such as happiness, peace, or joy.

Always research the properties of each herb and essential oil as they can irritate your skin if the wrong amount is added. Use a small amount of salve each time, avoiding any contact with your eyes, internal use, and keeping it out of reach of children.

You can store them in jars, tin cans, or any container that can be closed with a cap. Here is a general salve recipe you can follow for any type of salve you'd like to make:

1½ TEASPOONS BEESWAX	½ TABLESPOON COCONUT OIL (OPTIONAL)
¼ CUP OLIVE OIL (YOU CAN ALSO USE ALMOND OR JOJOBA)	4–8 DROPS OF ESSENTIAL OIL

1 Place your beeswax and the oil in the first of two empty glass jars. Set the jar in a saucepan with approximately 3 fingers of water. Turn the stove to low heat and let it slowly melt the beeswax.

2 Take the pan off the stove and carefully remove the jar. Dissolve the coconut oil if you decide to use it and then add the essential oil to the mixture in the jar.

3 When the mixture starts cooling down, the surface will start solidifying. Stir it with a chopstick and infuse your intent.

4 Once the mixture is cooled—but before it solidi-
fies—pour it into your second jar and seal it.

5 Remember to write down the ingredients and the
date you make it.

6 You can use it by rubbing it on your wrists, temples,
over your heart, or on your third eye.

Let's look into some different types of salves you
can make:

HAPPINESS SALVE: 2 drops of lavender, 2 drops
of rose, 1 drop of lemon

HEALING SALVE: Leave 2 to 3 handfuls of plantain
in a jar filled with olive oil. Let it rest in a dark space
for 3 to 4 weeks. Use the oil to create this magickal
salve. You can then add 2 drops of eucalyptus and
1 drop of peppermint. This salve is especially good
for coughs, irritated skin, and insect bites.

LOVE SALVE: 3 drops of jasmine, 2 drops of rose,
2 drops of violet, 1 drop of vanilla

PROSPERITY SALVE: 2 drops of thyme, 1 drop
of cinnamon, 2 drops of orange, 2 drops of mint

PURIFICATION SALVE: 2 drops of sandalwood,
3 drops of lavender, 2 drops of lemon balm

SLEEPING SALVE: 3 drops of lavender, 2 drops
of chamomile, 2 drops of valerian, 2 drops of rose

ESSENTIAL OILS

Essential oil is an oil that contains the essential essence of one or more herbs. The easiest way to create it is by maceration (page 81). Crafting an oil can be a perfect way to infuse our intent into a potion; this way it will already have our energies in it, contrary to an oil bought from a shop.

The great majority of Witches prefer to carry a natural product with them. Using essential oils is a guarantee that you're using the pure essence of the plant that was used. Essential oils must not be confused with perfume oils, as those are made artificially. Perfume oils are cheaper than essential oils—however, they don't carry the essence of an herb and for that reason, I don't advise using them for spells or rituals.

Essential oils are generally used to anoint objects; we will see in the last chapter how we can anoint a candle or other objects with them. You can also add them to a magick bath, sachets, and much more to strengthen their magickal powers.

Creating essential oils can also be a fun activity to boost your creativity and intuition. When you feel inspired you can add a drop or two onto your magickal tools, into a spell, or even on your skin if the herbs won't irritate it. Every time you use essential oils for magickal purposes, write down your feelings and observations to understand what combinations work and what don't.

As mentioned before, you can create many different combinations of essential oils, mixing them together to create your personal magick blend. There aren't specific rules for creating a personal blend: follow your intuition and base the mixture on the outcome you'd like to achieve.

We are now aware that each different herb and plant has specific properties that can help us manifest what we desire. When you have a goal in mind and you'd like to use essential oil to boost your powers to manifest something, write down on a piece of paper what you'd like to achieve. Once you know that, start researching what plants can help you, studying their magickal and medicinal attributes.

Create a list of plants that might be helpful—you can select up to ten different herbs and plants to create your personal blend. Even the quantity of each essential oil is up to you. Always be aware of the possibility of irritation or allergies, and carefully select the amount of each essential oil you will use. Pour the drops into a small glass bottle with a tiny dropper.

Once you've created your blend, hold the glass bottle and infuse your intent, imagining a white light coming from your hands into the blend. Seal the bottle properly and write a label with all the ingredients you've used and the date. Here are some ideas for different combinations:

HEALTH BLEND: 1 part eucalyptus, 1 part almond, 1 part ginger

PURIFICATION BLEND: 1 part sandalwood, 1 part lavender, ½ part mint, 1 part pine

PEACE BLEND: 1 part violet, 1 part lavender, 1 part hibiscus, 1 part apple

PROSPERITY BLEND: 1 part thyme, 1 part pine, ½ part almond, 1 part cinnamon

LOVE BLEND: 1 part jasmine, 1 part rose, 1 part hibiscus, 1 part valerian, ½ part vanilla

PROTECTION BLEND: 1 part clove, 1 part sage, 1 part rosemary, 1 part hazel

HERBAL INCENSE

Herbal incense is a nice way to enjoy the scent of our herbs and experience their magickal characteristics while being environmentally friendly. Incense sticks are very popular and easy to find. However, sometimes they might not be 100% natural, which can be unhealthy for us or our furry friends.

Herbal incense is a safe alternative, because we can decide which and how many types of herbs we'd like to use. We can make different kinds of incense for different purposes by utilizing our knowledge of the various attributes of plants.

All the herbs we decide to use must be dry. If we want to use herbs from our garden, we can dry them in the oven by following the steps on page 80. Before blending your herbs, it is very important to study them and know if they are what we're looking for. Some herbs are very toxic and breathing their smoke can cause serious damage to our bodies. Writing all these details down in our Book of Shadows (page 45) or journal can be helpful, so we won't forget what we learn day by day.

There's no specific rule that tells us the right amounts of herbs we should blend to create our incenses. Most of the magickal crafts are ruled by our intuition and needs. Base the amount of the ingredient on the purpose of the incense: if it's for happiness, concentrate more on the plant with that specific attribute. If you need one for meditating, concentrate on relaxing plants, and so on.

Once your herbs are dried and ready to be used, it is time to blend them. The blending process can vary depending on what tools you have in your house. You can blend your herbs with a mortar and pestle, a coffee grounder, or an electric blender.

When the herbs are blended, keep them in a sealed jar. Additionally, you can add some essential oils or resins to your herbs.

The mixture can be used immediately or stored for a few weeks. Many Witches bless the jar before using their incense to make sure all the energies contained in the jar are positive, and to boost their power. You can follow the following steps to bless your jar:

1   Hold the jar in your hands and take three to six deep breaths with a clear and calm mind.

2   Imagine a white light coming out of your hands and going into the jar, wrapping all the herbs inside it. Meditate for a few minutes on your intent and on what the incense is for.

3   Your jar is now blessed and ready to be used.

It is now time to burn our blend and enjoy its magickal smoke. To burn our blend, we will need some self-igniting charcoal (different from BBQ charcoal); a fireproof plate filled with sand, soil, or stones; and a lighter. Your charcoal has to be at least one inch long. It will then burn for a little less than an hour.

Hold your charcoal briquette with tweezers and light it with your lighter; always be careful to not hurt yourself when using flames. In the beginning, when the charcoal comes into contact with the flame, it will start sparking. When you can see the sparks across almost the whole surface, place the charcoal on your fireproof plate. If you want to be extra safe, cover your table with a heatproof cloth or material.

The briquette will be ready when its color is an incandescent red.

You are now ready to add your incense blend. The perfect amount to use each time is one teaspoon. As an incense stick burns gradually on its own when you use an herb blend, if you pour too much mixture onto the charcoal, a big cloud of smoke might occur, and your incense will burn very quickly. To enjoy the nice perfume and avoid too much smoke, sprinkle the blend onto the charcoal gradually. Although it might not seem like enough, remember that in this case, less is more.

When the incense is finished, wait for ten to fifteen minutes until all the smoke goes away, then sprinkle more incense onto the charcoal. At the end, leave the briquette to burn; it will turn into ash when finished. Never throw the ash in the trash as soon as you finish burning the incense, as some sparks of fire might still be present. I advise leaving the ash in a fireproof place for a day to be sure all the fire is gone.

Here are some ideas for your herbal incenses:

ABUNDANCE: thyme, basil, cinnamon, vanilla

HAPPINESS: orange, frankincense, hibiscus

PURIFICATION: sandalwood, mint, lemon

PEACE: lavender, violet, jasmine

LOVE: rose, lavender, apple, chamomile

MEDITATION: frankincense, clove, lavender

CHAPTER 6

CRAFTING IN YOUR KITCHEN

The act of eating is considered to be sacred in many religions. Connecting with what we eat is extremely important for our body and soul. In modern society, many people try to spend a minimal amount of time in their kitchen, always trying to find the quickest way to prepare a meal. With the speed of our world, it is sometimes difficult to find the time to sit down and enjoy our meals.

Despite our busy routines, spending time preparing our food, caring about each ingredient, and taking all the time we need to cook tasty and healthy food is an act of kindness we do for ourselves. The ingredients we carefully choose to create our meals with bring with them specific energies that our body will absorb, and that will not only affect the physical body but the spiritual one as well.

Bringing awareness into our kitchen is a beneficial magickal practice that will massively improve our lives. Here are some magickal associations for different types of food, followed by a discussion on how we could prepare them.

VEGETABLES

ASPARAGUS: passion

AUBERGINE: manifestation, wealth

BEAN: family, love, harmony

BEET: love

CABBAGE: fertility, good luck, money

CARROT: lust, fertility

CAULIFLOWER: glamour, calm

CELERY: psychic abilities, lust

CUCUMBER: healing

LEEK: love, protection, strength

LETTUCE: divination, sleep, protection, love

MUSHROOM: psychic awareness, grounding

ONION: stability, prosperity, protection

PEA: money, luck

POTATO: money, luck, healing

PUMPKIN: lunar magick, prosperity, protection

RADISH: protection, lust

SPINACH: money, fortitude, health, strength

TOMATO: protection, love, creativity

ZUCCHINI: passion, protection, spirituality

FRUITS

APPLE: love, friendship, healing, longevity

APRICOT: love

AVOCADO: beauty, love, attraction

BANANA: fertility, potency, prosperity

BERGAMOT: money, improving memory, sleep

BLUEBERRY: protection, peace, abundance

CHERRY: love, happiness, divination

COCONUT: protection, purification

CRANBERRY: protection, healing

FIG: divination, fertility, love

GRAPE: fertility, money, garden magick

KIWI: love, fidelity

LEMON: cleansing, purification, health

OLIVE: fidelity, marriage, money, peace

ORANGE: health, happiness, purification

PEACH: wisdom, love, harmony

PINEAPPLE: luck, memory, prosperity

PLUM: healing, peace, love

RASPBERRY: courage, healing

STRAWBERRY: success, good luck

TANGERINE: energy, vitality, strength

FRUIT RECIPES

LOVE FRUIT SALAD

Fruits are delicious on their own, and a combination of them can be a very healthy and tasty snack or dessert. This fruit salad is created with the intent of bringing more love into our lives or others'. You can determine the amounts of the ingredients, using your intuition to create magickal dishes in your kitchen.

PEACHES

APPLES
(PREFERABLY RED)

CHERRIES (PITTED)

LEMON JUICE
OF HALF A LEMON

SUGAR

1 Cut the peaches, apples, and cherries into slices and combine them in a bowl. Make sure there are no seeds left in your bowl.

2 Add some lemon juice. With a medium-size bowl, I advise using half a lemon.

3 Sprinkle some sugar on top and mix well. Infuse your intent by placing your hands on top of the bowl, with your palms facing down, while meditating.

4 Leave the fruit salad to rest in your fridge for one hour.

PROSPERITY FRUIT SALAD

This salad is made with the intent of attracting more money. After a meditation session or after journaling, enjoy this salad and light a green candle to boost your manifestation.

BLUEBERRIES

STRAWBERRIES

PINEAPPLE

APPLES

THYME

LEMON JUICE, TO TASTE

SUGAR

1   Dice all your fruits, place them in a bowl, and make sure there are no seeds left.

2   Add thyme (can be fresh or dried) and lemon juice to your bowl and sprinkle some sugar on top. Mix well.

3   Infuse your intent by placing your hands on top of the bowl, with your palms facing down, while meditating.

4   Leave the fruit salad to rest in the fridge for one hour.

MAGICKAL PIE TO ATTRACT PEACE AND GOOD LUCK

This is a simple fruit pie made with the intent of attracting peace and good luck. It is a cozy snack to eat at any time of year. If you can't find fresh strawberries, you can use frozen ones; just remember to defrost them at least six hours before using them.

FOR THE CRUST

4–5 TABLESPOONS
COLD WATER
(DEPENDING ON
WHAT TYPE OF
FLOUR YOU USE)

2 EGG YOLKS

2 CUPS FLOUR

10 TABLESPOONS
COLD BUTTER

1 TEASPOON SALT

1½ TABLESPOONS
SUGAR

½ TEASPOON
CINNAMON

FOR THE FILLING

2 CUPS
STRAWBERRIES

⅓ CUP SUGAR

1 TABLESPOON
CORNSTARCH

LEMON JUICE AND
LEMON ZEST OF
1 LEMON

A PINCH OF SALT

FOR THE TOPPING

1 EGG

SUGAR

BASIL

1   Mix the cold water with the eggs yolks and set it aside.

2   Mix the flour and the cold butter with your fingers.

3   Add the salt, sugar, and cinnamon.

4   Incorporate the cold water and egg yolks into
    the mixture.

5   Once it's all mixed together, form a ball, wrap it
    in cling film, and leave it to rest in the fridge for
    one hour.

6   For the filling, cut your strawberries into thin slices
    and place them in a bowl.

7   Add the sugar, cornstarch, lemon juice and zest, and
    a pinch of salt. Mix well and leave in the refrigerator
    for at least one hour.

8 Once the appropriate time has passed, roll out the dough, forming a circle. Make sure the dough is not too thick or it will be hard to eat. Keep in mind that you don't need a pan for this pie.

9 Pour the strawberry mix in the middle of the circle and gently fold the dough towards the inside.

10 Brush some egg on the dough and sprinkle some sugar on top of the strawberries and the dough.

11 Place the pie in the oven at 450°F for 25 minutes.

12 Once it's ready, place some fresh basil on top. Once it has cooled down, enjoy!

FRUIT DRINKS

Fruits can be used to create tasty and hydrating beverages, perfect to drink on a hot summer day. These recipes are quick and easy and don't make much of a mess.

For example, you could make nice flavored waters; water has the magickal power to absorb the energies around it. That's why it is common to put crystals (only the ones that are not dangerous for our body—please make sure to use the right ones) in a jar of water to then be drank.

You can also make healthy and delicious smoothies with fruits and dairy. Dairy has the power to attract abundance, prosperity, and love. If you're in possession of a juicer, you can make simple juices with a combination of different fruits; you might want to add just a little bit of lemon or lime juice to bring out the flavor.

HAPPINESS-FLAVORED WATER

This is a simple recipe to make our water taste more interesting and bring more happiness into our lives. This can be an excellent solution if you're struggling to drink enough water and you're looking for a pleasant way to hydrate your body. You can keep the quantities indicated in this recipe and change the ingredients if you'd like to create a different kind of magick water.

1 LITER STILL WATER

4-6 STRAWBERRIES

4-6 SLICES OF LEMON

4 SLICES OF LIME

4 FRESH MINT LEAVES

1   Pour one liter of still water in a jug.

2   Cut the strawberries into little chunks.

3   Pour the fruit into the jug and add your mint leaves.

4   Leave the jug in the fridge for at least 30 minutes; this way the water will have time to absorb all the flavors.

5   You can then drink your water, or add some ice cubes before consuming. Enjoy!

VEGAN SMOOTHIE FOR CLEANSING

This smoothie recipe is suitable for anyone that doesn't include dairy in their diet. You can substitute the fruit juice with water for a thin result, or dairy (milk or yogurt) for a thicker one.

½ APPLE

½ CUP MIXED BERRIES

GINGER (DEPENDING ON HOW STRONG YOU'D LIKE IT)

LEMON JUICE, TO TASTE

¼ CUP OF FRUIT JUICE, LIKE GRAPE OR PEAR (WATER FOR A LIGHTER SMOOTHIE, DAIRY FOR A THICKER SMOOTHIE)

1   Cut your apple, berries, and ginger into small chunks.

2   Place the fruit chunks in your blender and add the lemon juice and the fruit juice.

3   Blend all the ingredients until smooth.

4   Enjoy your smoothie with some ice and garnish with fresh fruit.

MAGICK SYRUPS

Syrups are a good alternative to honey or other sweeteners. You can use them to garnish toasts, ice creams, and other desserts.

They are very simple to make, and adding different herbs or fruits can infuse their magickal attributes.

ELDERBERRY SYRUP

Elderberry syrup is a common concoction, especially in the Witchy community. Elderberries contain vitamins A, B, and C, which stimulate our immune system. You can dissolve the syrup in a cup of hot water when you have a cold or flu. I use honey to achieve a thick consistency, but for a lighter consistency you can just add water. In this recipe, I use dried elderberries, as they might be easier to find. If you can find fresh ones, just double the amount you use.

3½ CUPS WATER

⅔ CUP DRIED ELDERBERRIES

½ TEASPOON CINNAMON

2 TABLESPOONS GINGER

½ TEASPOON GROUND CLOVES

1 CUP HONEY

1   Pour the water into a saucepan and then add the elderberries, cinnamon, ginger, and ground cloves.

2   Bring to a boil over medium heat. Once the mixture is boiling, set the heat to low for 45 minutes to 1 hour.

3   Mash the berries and strain the syrup to make sure there aren't any full pieces of fruit left.

4   Pour the syrup into a glass jar and let it cool down.

5   Seal the jar. Enjoy your syrup!

LAVENDER SYRUP

This syrup is perfect for many different occasions. You can dissolve it in your chamomile before going to bed to achieve peaceful sleep, or you can add it to a nice lemon sorbet, as the flavor of lavender goes very well with citrus. Not only will its magickal color surprise any guests you invite to dinner, but it will bring them happiness, peace, love, tranquility, purification, protection, and healing from grief.

1 CUP WATER   1 CUP LAVENDER

1 CUP SUGAR

1   Pour the water into a saucepan, then add the sugar and lavender.

2   Bring to a boil and stir until all the sugar dissolves.

3   Let it rest for 30 minutes.

4   Strain and pour the syrup into a glass jar and seal.

VEGETABLE RECIPES

Like fruits, vegetables carry magickal properties that can turn your dishes into a magickal experience. To connect more with the season and nature, you can pick your vegetables according to the seasonal cycle and, when possible, support local vegetable stores.

A combination of seasonal vegetables and vegetables with the magickal associations you need will make your meals powerful—and healthy.

CHICKWEED PESTO

Chickweed is a very powerful medicinal plant, rich in vitamins A, B, and C, with the magickal association of healing. This pesto can be used as a pasta sauce, for sandwiches, or as a topping. If you'd like to store it, you can create some "ice cubes" of pesto to keep in the freezer.

3 CUPS CHICKWEED

2 GARLIC CLOVES

½ CUP WATER

½ CUP OLIVE OIL

½ CUP PINE NUTS

1 TABLESPOON NUTRITIONAL YEAST

½ CUP PARMESAN

SALT AND PEPPER, TO TASTE

1   Wash your chickweed under fresh, cold water.

2   Place the chickweed in a blender and add the garlic, water, oil, pine nuts, nutritional yeast, cheese, and salt and pepper, to taste. Blend everything.

3   Enjoy your pesto with some pasta, on a sandwich, or as a dipping sauce.

CREAM OF PUMPKIN AND ROSEMARY

This creamy soup is a cozy, autumn–winter meal, perfect to bring prosperity, protection, healing, and longevity. You can serve it as a meal, accompanied by a toasted slice of bread.

1 SMALL ONION

2 GARLIC CLOVES

1 CARROT

1 BUNCH OF CELERY

½ CUP OLIVE OIL

1 SMALL PUMPKIN
(3 TO 4 POUNDS)

4 CUPS VEGETABLE
BROTH

2–3 TABLESPOONS
COCONUT MILK

A FEW SPRIGS OF
ROSEMARY

NUTMEG, TO TASTE

CUMIN, TO TASTE

SALT AND PEPPER,
TO TASTE

1. Chop the onion, garlic, carrot, and celery into small pieces.

2. Pour the oil into your pan and set the stove to low heat.

3. Add the mix of veggies you chopped and sauté for 3–4 minutes.

4. Clean your pumpkin and cut it into little cubes. Add it to the pan and let it cook for another 3–4 minutes.

5. Add the vegetable broth and set to medium heat. Let it cook for 20 minutes.

6   Add the coconut milk, rosemary, nutmeg, cumin, salt, and pepper. If you still have some chunks of pumpkin, you can mash them with a fork or a potato masher. Let it cook for 10–15 minutes.

7   At this point, you should have a creamy pumpkin sauce, ready to be served. You can garnish with a trickle of coconut oil and some rosemary.

HERBAL BREAD

This herbal bread is a perfect recipe to bring abundance, prosperity, and health into your life. As the recipe mostly relies on the power of the herbs, try to use fresh ones.

4-5 TEASPOONS ACTIVE DRY YEAST

2 CUPS WARM WATER

1½ TABLESPOONS WHITE SUGAR

1 TABLESPOON SALT

5-6 CUPS FLOUR, PLUS MORE FOR KNEADING

¼ CUP OLIVE OIL

1 TEASPOON GARLIC POWDER

1 TABLESPOON CHOPPED ROSEMARY

1 TABLESPOON CHOPPED THYME

1 TABLESPOON CHOPPED DILL

1 TEASPOON CHOPPED CHIVES

1 TEASPOON CHOPPED OREGANO

1   Mix the yeast in a cup of warm water with sugar. Leave it until it becomes foamy.

2 In a bowl, mix the salt with the flour. Slowly add the yeast mixture, while kneading, and add the rest of the water.

3 Gradually add the oil, garlic powder, and all your chopped herbs.

4 Knead for about 10 minutes, until the dough is smooth. You can add more flour if needed.

5 Punch the dough a few times to release all the air, then form two balls that you will leave to rest on an oily surface, covered with a clean, damp cloth.

6 Let them rest for approximately one hour until they double in size.

7 Sprinkle some flour on a surface and knead each ball for about 5 minutes.

8 Brush the tops with olive oil and let them rest until they reach the size you desire.

9 Heat the oven to 400°F and bake your bread for 15 minutes.

10 You can enjoy this bread with some butter, a nice pesto (page 104), or some grilled vegetables.

TEA MAGICK

Tea is a very common drink. It is very versatile, as you can appreciate it hot or cold. It's normally made with hot water and different variations of herbs, flowers, or fruits. It takes very little time to make. The variety in different herb combinations is infinite, and therefore so are the magickal purposes for these teas.

You can combine different types of herbs based on your desires and what you want to bring into your life. Teas are also used as a medicinal remedy, as they can help us to take care of our body and soul. However, these recipes are not meant to substitute real medicines; always research what's best for you and consult your doctor regarding any medical issues.

For Witches, tea is not only an enjoyable drink, but it can be an important part of rituals, as its magickal powers can enhance the energies of a spell or help us to get in contact with spirits. In these recipes, I'll use dried flowers and herbs; if you'd like to use fresh ones, double the amounts you use.

If you'd like to create a tea blend that lasts for more than one serving, you just have to store the blending in a sealed jar. Always remember to write down all the ingredients and the date on a label.

HEADACHE REMEDY TEA

This tea is intended to cure headaches. Once it's ready, inhale the steam and enjoy the drink. Keep the blend in a sealed jar; use one tablespoon for each serving. It is important to let it brew for 5 minutes.

1 TABLESPOON
LAVENDER

2 TABLESPOONS
CHAMOMILE

½ TABLESPOON MINT

1 TEASPOON
TURMERIC

1 TEASPOON GINGER

1   Mix all the herbs in a jar.

2   Fill your teacup with boiling water and brew
    1 tablespoon of the tea blend.

3   Wait 5–10 minutes before drinking.

PSYCHIC TEA

This tea is specifically made to help your psychic
work. As mentioned in previous chapters, you can
incorporate some divination and crystallomancy
techniques into your practice. Drinking this tea
before those sorts of practices can help you enhance
your powers.

6 TABLESPOONS
ROSE PETALS

4 TABLESPOONS
THYME

4 TEASPOONS
YARROW ROOT

2 TEASPOONS
CINNAMON

2 TEASPOONS CLOVES

1   Mix your herbs in a jar. Hold it in your hands,
    imagine a white light coming from your head all the
    way down to your hands, into the jar. Infuse your
    desires and ask the herbs to aid you in your intent.

2 Boil a cup of water, then add 1 tablespoon of the tea blend.

3 Let it brew for 5–10 minutes. Inhale the steam and enjoy the drink.

SLEEP TEA

This tea will bring you peace, tranquility, balance, healing, and love. All these magickal attributes will help you settle into a peaceful sleep.

4 TABLESPOONS CHAMOMILE

2 TABLESPOONS LAVENDER

3 TABLESPOONS CATNIP

1 Mix your herbs in a glass jar.

2 Boil a cup of water, add 1 tablespoon of the tea blend, and let it brew for 5-10 minutes.

3 You can add a teaspoon of honey if you'd like a sweeter flavor. Enjoy your drink before bedtime.

LOVE TEA

This tea will help you bring more love into your life or boost the one you already have. That love can be directed toward yourself or another person. Its magickal associations are love, peace, tranquility, and happiness.

3 TABLESPOONS ROSE PETALS

2 TABLESPOONS JASMINE

3 TABLESPOONS HIBISCUS

½ TEASPOON CINNAMON

1 Mix your herbs in a glass jar.

2 Boil a cup of water, add 1 tablespoon of the tea blend, and let it brew for 5-10 minutes.

3 Inhale the steam of the tea and enjoy.

MEDITATION TEA

This tea helps you concentrate and focus during a meditation session. Drink it twenty minutes before meditating for a clear and focused mind.

4 TABLESPOONS ENGLISH BREAKFAST TEA

1 TABLESPOONS ROSE HIPS

2 TABLESPOONS ELDERFLOWER

1 BRANCH OF ROSEMARY

1 Mix your herbs in a glass jar. Spend some time infusing your desires and intent, asking the herbs to help you have a peaceful meditation session.

2 Boil a cup of water, add 1 tablespoon of the tea blend, and let it brew for 5-10 minutes.

3 Inhale the steam and enjoy the tea.

CHAPTER 7

SPELLS AND CHARMS

The art of spellworking is a practice that helps you focus and achieve what you want from life by using a combination of your energies and the energies of nature. By channeling your powers into one aspect, which can be money, love, protection, happiness, etc., you're able to manipulate the energy of the universe to get the result you wish for.

Casting spells is an important practice for us Witches, as it requires a strong connection with nature and planet Earth in order to perform them successfully. Keep in mind at the beginning of your practice—but also if you are an old practitioner—that it is absolutely normal that not all your spells bring results. Sometimes we must work on the perfect recipe, other times we must put more effort into balancing our energies. For a spell to be successful it requires knowledge, experience, practice, and patience.

If a spell doesn't work it can signify two reasons. The first one is that we did something wrong or our energies weren't used properly; in this case, it is advised that you wait at least three weeks before trying again. Many people use magick for greed, which can be dangerous and will turn your practice into unproductive work. Another reason can be that the spell wasn't meant to work. We often want things from life that simply aren't meant to happen.

One of the main principles in magick is that if you can obtain something without using magick then you shouldn't use it. When you perform a spell, remember that has to be followed by concrete actions. If you perform a love spell to attract a new person into your life, you'll have to go out and meet new people. In that case, your spell will help you with your intent; otherwise, it will be in vain.

Another principle everyone should follow is to never hurt other people. Some call it black magick; others don't like to make a distinction. However, it is absolutely not a good idea to try and hurt others by performing a spell. Remember that when you put negative energies into the universe, they will eventually come back to you. Always respect others and nature.

Reciting a formula, creating a potion, or performing a ritual with magick tools are all to be considered spells. Spells can also be divided into categories: blessing, evocation, celebration, and banishing.

BLESSING: When you buy a new object or a house, or before a ritual, you might want to do a blessing spell. Depending on the situation, you can perform a whole ritual or simply bestow your blessing with incense, a candle, or some herbs.

EVOCATION: This type of spell is performed when you want to attract something or someone into your life. This is the most common spell in the Witchy community, as it is used to improve our lives by inviting new feelings, aspects, or situations.

CELEBRATION: This sort of spell/ritual is normally dedicated to celebrating the moon, the seasons, the deities, or other types of spirits. You can perform it at any time of the month and year. It is also used to dedicate an altar to whomever you want to celebrate.

BANISHING: This spell is the opposite of an evocation spell. It is performed to remove something from our life. It is very difficult to establish if it's necessary to completely remove something from our lives. Think carefully before performing this spell, and if you're in doubt, resort to an evocation spell.

Below are a few combinations of elements that you can use on different occasions, depending on your goals. Keep in mind that this is only to help you create your personal spells; there are no specific rules to follow, so feel free to experiment and find the ingredients and elements that work best for you.

LOVE AND RELATIONSHIP-RELATED SPELLS

BEST DAY:
FRIDAY

ELEMENT(S):
WATER, EARTH

PLANET:
VENUS

COLOR(S):
PINK, RED, GREEN

HERBS:
ROSES, HIBISCUS, MINT, APPLE, VERBENA, THYME, LAVENDER

CRYSTALS:
LAPIS LAZULI, TOPAZ, CARNELIAN, RHODOCHROSITE

JOB-RELATED SPELLS

BEST DAY:
SUNDAY

ELEMENT(S):
FIRE

PLANET:
SUN

COLOR(S):
YELLOW, ORANGE

HERBS:
CHAMOMILE, CALENDULA, MINT, ROSE, MARJORAM

CRYSTALS:
CAT'S EYE, GREEN AVENTURINE, CITRINE

PROTECTION AND HOME PROTECTION-RELATED SPELLS

BEST DAY:
SATURDAY

ELEMENT(S):
WATER, EARTH

PLANET:
SATURN

COLOR(S):
BLACK

HERBS:
CYPRESS, ROSEMARY, DILL, EUCALYPTUS, GARLIC, LEMON, MARJORAM, MUGWORT, PARSLEY, SAGE

CRYSTALS:
AMETHYST, BLACK TOURMALINE, OBSIDIAN, SMOKY QUARTZ

CREATIVITY-RELATED SPELLS

BEST DAY:
WEDNESDAY

ELEMENT(S):
AIR, WATER

PLANET:
MERCURY

COLOR(S):
PURPLE, VIOLET, GREEN

HERBS:
SANDALWOOD, LAVENDER, CUMIN, VALERIAN, VANILLA

CRYSTALS:
CLEAR QUARTZ, TIGER'S EYE, FLUORITE, LAPIS LAZULI

PROSPERITY-RELATED SPELLS

BEST DAY:
THURSDAY

ELEMENT(S):
AIR, FIRE

PLANET:
JUPITER

COLOR(S):
BLUE, GREEN, PURPLE

HERBS:
SAGE, THYME, MINT,
BASIL, PARSLEY,
GINGER

CRYSTALS:
GREEN JADE,
PYRITE, CITRINE,
GREEN AVENTURINE

COURAGE AND PASSION-RELATED SPELLS

BEST DAY:
TUESDAY

ELEMENT(S):
FIRE

PLANET:
MARS

COLOR(S):
RED

HERBS:
ROSE, HIBISCUS,
CHILI PEPPER,
BASIL, ALOE, AND
CORIANDER

CRYSTALS:
HEMATITE, RED
JASPER, WATERMELON
TOURMALINE,
CARNELIAN

INTUITION AND FEMININE ENERGY-RELATED SPELLS

BEST DAY:
MONDAY

ELEMENT(S):
WATER

PLANET:
MOON

COLOR(S):
WHITE, SILVER, GRAY

HERBS:
BERGAMOT, MUGWORT, CLOVES, DILL, ROWAN, PATCHOULI, SAGE

CRYSTALS:
SELENITE, MOONSTONE, CLEAR QUARTZ

WHAT'S THE DIFFERENCE BETWEEN A SPELL AND A CHARM?

Charms are included under the umbrella of spells. When we perform a spell, we can give power to an object, a tool, or a piece of jewelry. When a specific object gains power through a spell, we call that object a charm.

For example, you can perform a spell on a special necklace you have, turning that necklace into an object that will protect you from negative energies.

In that case, your necklace becomes a magick charm. Even a specific word that contains magickal properties can be considered a charm, normally with a positive connotation.

SIGILS

A sigil is a particular symbol created to represent a specific goal or concept. Not only Witches and Pagans, but also many ancient civilizations used sigils in their culture to represent different aspects of life. They were commonly used to represent or honor deities and spirits. In the modern world, the majority of sigils are created to attract more wealth, happiness, love, and other aspects and intentions.

Sigils are a form of art used to symbolize an aspect that we'd like to bring into our lives. When used in magickal arts, sigils absorb all energies and powers. It can be difficult to externalize our desires simply through the power of our mind; that's why sigils are a powerful form of magick that help us to concretize what we'd like to achieve.

Sigils can be drawn in many different places—in fact, anywhere that connects with our goal. You can draw them on candles, tools, books, pots, jewelry, on the soil under your gardening tool(s), jars, and so on. Although they are very powerful, they can't be used as a substitute for a spell and concrete actions.

The first thing you need to think about if you'd like to create your own sigils is your intention. What would you like to achieve? What is your primary intent? When you decide what you'd like to get from your sigils, write it down on a piece of paper.

For example:

"I WANT TO FIND A GOOD JOB."

Now cancel all the vowels and the letters that repeat themselves.

"W N T F D G J B"

Deconstruct the letters that are left and draw every single line or curve. Using the lines and curves, create a symbol that is meaningful to you. By following these steps, you will create your personal sigils. Infuse your energies into the sigils to be sure they will work and contain your desires and intent.

Once the sigil is created, you'll need to activate it to make it work and send the energy into the universe. There are two methods you can use:

ACTIVE ACTIVATION: This type of activation is good when you want a quick and immediate result. For example, you might use an active activation if you want to manifest something or create a situation in the near future. In this case, you need to create your sigil and destroy it: the destruction will free all the energies that the sigil was keeping in the universe. You can do so by drawing a sigil on a piece of paper and dissolving it in water. Alternatively, you can draw a sigil on a piece of paper and then burn it.

PASSIVE ACTIVATION: This type of activation is used when you want the energies of the sigil to last for a long period of time. For example, you can use this method if you'd like to be protected from bad luck or if you'd like to invite more happiness and peace.

Here you'll have to draw your sigil onto an object or carve it on a candle or other object. It is important that you not destroy it, but leave it as it is instead.

WRITE YOUR OWN SPELLS

It is not always easy to find already-written spells that suit our intent. Most of the time, it is best if we write our own spells. This way the spell will be more powerful and perfectly designed for what we want to attract.

If you don't have time or you can't write one, however, don't feel discouraged. A spell written by another Witch might work just fine. But when you are about to write a spell yourself, you want to take into consideration these things:

INTENTION: The intention is the foundation of a spell. Without a clear intent, a spell will never work. Think carefully about what you want to achieve: think about the details, the outcome, and the possible consequences. Can I achieve this goal without using magick? Is it worth it? How will I feel when I achieve it? Will I hurt or upset anyone? Once your ideas are clear, it can be helpful to write down your intent.

TOOLS AND INGREDIENTS: You want to think about what kind of spell you'd like to perform and what material(s) you need. Organize the necessary herbs, flowers, and tools you'll need. This way, when it's time to perform the spell, everything will be ready and you won't run out of time or risk postponing the whole ritual.

WHEN: The time you perform your spell is very important, as each day or lunar cycle brings with it different energies (page 38). Based on the outcome you desire, carefully choose the perfect moment to perform your spell.

CASTING MOMENT: When you're about to perform your spell, double-check that everything is near you and ready to be used. Remember to cleanse all the tools and ingredients, and if needed, cleanse yourself as well. Think about protecting your aura by performing a protection spell or closing a magick circle. If you've considered your intention, gathered your tools and ingredients, chosen the perfect moment, and ensured that you and your materials are cleansed and prepared, you'll be ready to perform your personal spell.

DIFFERENT TYPES OF SPELLS

There are many different ways to perform a spell. All of them allow you to manipulate, direct, and change various energies. No particular spell is more powerful than another—what matters is how you do it and the strength of your magickal powers. However, you might discover that your powers are stronger when performing a specific type of spell.

Feel free to experiment with different types of spells. Don't be scared of making mistakes, as that is the only way to get experience and find out what type of magick is most suitable for you. The main ways to perform spells are spell jars, candle spells, and spray spells.

SPELL JARS

These spells are made using a physical glass jar or container that can be sealed. A magick jar will contain all the power brought by the different ingredients you use and put inside it. It can be made with herbs, crystals, flowers, sigils, pieces of paper with your intent written on them, and more. It is advised that you only use dried herbs and flowers; fresh ones might create mold pretty quickly.

Before adding the ingredients to the jar, you can do a quick cleanse of each item with Palo Santo. Remember to infuse your intent to the jar by holding it and spending some time meditating on your intentions. Once the jar is filled with your magickal ingredients and sealed with a cap, pick a candle with a color related to your intent and let the candle burn on top of the jar; the wax will seal the jar and boost its power.

A spell jar can be kept in almost any place, depending on its size. You can keep it in your bag, hang it in your car, leave it on a table in your house, or hang it on a window. The power of the jar could fade after a while; this depends on your intuition and feelings.

When the spell is over, you can open the jar and return all the natural elements to nature. If you've used a crystal, you can cleanse it and use it again. As for the jar, don't leave it in nature or bury it; it's bad for the environment. You can use it again or recycle it.

SOME IDEAS FOR SPELLS JARS

HOME PROTECTION: Use black tourmaline, rosemary, cinnamon, lavender, and salt. Seal with a black candle.

CREATIVITY: Use lapis lazuli, chamomile, cinnamon, cumin, a piece of paper with your intent, and salt. Seal with a green candle.

ABUNDANCE: Use citrine, basil, thyme, mint, and some coins or a banknote. Seal with a purple candle.

HAPPINESS: Use clear quartz, jasmine, rose water, hibiscus, and a piece of paper with your intent written on it. Seal with a yellow candle.

INTUITION: Use moonstone, mugwort, sage (or sage oil), and bergamot (or bergamot oil). Seal with a white candle.

SELF-LOVE: Use rose quartz, rose petals, lavender, and patchouli. Seal with a pink candle.

CANDLE SPELLS

This is the most accessible way to perform spells, and can be very powerful. You will see many Witches performing candle spells, as they are simple and represent all four elements at once: the fire is represented by the flame, the water is represented by the melted wax, the air is represented by the air the candle needs to burn, and the earth is represented by the solid wax.

Just lighting a candle with intent can be considered a spell. However, you can boost its energies by adding more magick. You can decide to anoint a candle with an essential oil chosen based on your intent, you can pick a candle of a specific color, or you can add dried herbs and flowers by warming the wax and sticking the leaves to it. You can even decide to use all those methods.

You can also carve a sigil onto the candle and burn a piece of paper with your intent written on it. Don't feel obligated to use all of these methods—your spell will work even with a simple candle. However, these methods might help you to enhance the power of the spell.

A common question is how long a candle should burn. Others might suggest that you let it burn for a specific amount of time. However, I advise you to never blow out a candle spell but to let it burn until the end instead. Keep in mind that if you have to leave your house, it is not safe to leave a candle burning without supervision. In this scenario, blow the candle out and light it again when you can keep an eye on it.

SOME IDEAS FOR CANDLE SPELLS

CANDLE SPELL TO ATTRACT MONEY

This spell will help you attract more money into your life. It is advised that you practice some manifestation techniques: for example, journaling or meditating. It is important to take concrete actions in addition to this spell.

A GREEN CANDLE

OLIVE OIL

1 TEASPOON
CHILI PEPPER

1 TEASPOON THYME

1 TEASPOON MINT

1 TEASPOON
CINNAMON

1 Pour approximately two fingers of olive oil into a jar.

2 Add 1 teaspoon of each ingredient and mix well.

3 Let the mixture rest for at least three days. You can also charge it under the Full Moon or with the smoke of Palo Santo.

4 Anoint the candle with the magick oil you made and infuse your intent.

5 Light the candle and let it burn.

ANTI-ANXIETY CANDLE SPELL

This spell will help ease anxiety in your life. It can be done while drinking a nice Meditation Tea (page 111). This spell is not meant to substitute any medicine or medical prescription.

A PURPLE CANDLE   CHAMOMILE

LAVENDER

1   Warm the body of the candle with a small flame. When the wax is warm, sprinkle some dried lavender and chamomile onto it.

2   Spend some time meditating and infusing your intent into the candle.

3   Light it and let it burn.

LOVE CANDLE SPELL

One of the most requested spells is a love candle spell. By doing this spell, you increase your chances of finding new love. You can enjoy a nice Love tea (page 110) or Love salve (page 84) along with this spell.

A RED CANDLE   ROSE PETALS

HIBISCUS PETALS   SUGAR

1   Warm the body of the candle with a small flame. When the wax is warm, sprinkle the hibiscus and rose petals onto it.

2   Use the sugar to create a circle surrounding the candle.

3   Spend some time meditating and infusing your intent into the candle. After lighting the candle, sprinkle some sugar on top of it while imagining what you'd like your new love to look like.

4   Let the candle burn.

CANDLE SPELL TO BANISH BAD ENERGY

This candle spell is designed to send away all the bad energies that surround you. If the bad energies are in your house, I advise that you practice this spell in the center of your home.

A BLACK CANDLE   SALT

A PEN   CINNAMON

1   Carve a protection sigil or a pentagram onto the candle.

2   Light the candle and use salt to create a circle surrounding it.

3   Meditate and imagine all the bad energies leaving, driven away by the powerful energy of the candle.

4   Sprinkle some cinnamon on top of the salt circle.

5   Let the candle burn. Enjoy the pleasant sensation of the absence of bad energies around you, creating a feeling of gratitude.

SPRAY SPELLS

Spray spells are a magnificent and quick way to create some magick when needed. To create a spray spell, you start with a base of water and then add essential oils or herbs. Fill a spray bottle with room temperature water, add the drops of essential oil(s), and shake the bottle well.

If you want to use magick herbs, you'll have to boil some water, add your herbs, and let them simmer for a minimum of 10 minutes on low heat. When the water has cooled down, you can pour it into your spray bottle and use it when need it. The spray won't last more than 10 days if you use herbs. You can also use moon water to make the spray more powerful.

SOME IDEAS FOR SPRAY SPELLS

SPRAY SPELL TO REMOVE NEGATIVITY

This spray will help you to get rid of bad energies in a short amount of time. Keep it near you and use it when needed.

WATER

2 TABLESPOONS
ROSEMARY

1 TABLESPOON
HIMALAYAN SALT

A SPRAY BOTTLE

1   Bring the water to a boil and add the rosemary, approximately two tablespoons. Let it simmer for 10 minutes on low heat.

2   Add the Himalayan salt, and mix well until it dissolves. Spend some time meditating and infusing your intent.

3   Pour the spell into a spray bottle. If you want, you can add some more Himalayan salt before closing the bottle.

4   Spray it around you when you feel you are surrounded by negative energies.

GLAMOUR SPRAY

This spray can be used on your body, on your clothes, and on your makeup. It will boost your self-confidence and beauty.

MOON WATER

A SPRAY BOTTLE

ROSE ESSENTIAL OIL

CALENDULA ESSENTIAL OIL

ORANGE ESSENTIAL OIL

1   Pour some moon water into your spray bottle.

2   Add approximately 2 drops of rose, calendula, and orange essential oils.

3   Meditate and infuse your intent.

4   Use the spray when needed.

OTHER MAGICKAL SPELLS

In this last section of the book, I'll be sharing other methods and ways to perform spells. We've learned that in Witchcraft there aren't strict rules we must follow; take these spells as an inspiration or guide to understand how a spell is made. Feel free to create your own spells and experiment with more ways to perform magick.

Always keep in mind that everything done in spellcraft is energy work, where you share your energies with the universe. If you put bad intents and negative energies into the universe, these will eventually come back to you. To be protected from this, always cast a protection spell or use a magick circle. Always be careful: everything has a consequence. Keep in mind that it is important to pay great respect to others and nature.

BATH GLAMOUR SPELL

When you feel down and need a boost of self-esteem, perform this bath spell to help take care of your body and mind. Baths are a perfect time to relax and grow your self-love.

This spell won't cause any negative effects. However, if you perform it with a negative attitude, it can bring out the things you hate most in yourself. If you work with deities, I strongly advise leaving an offering for the goddess Aphrodite.

The offering can be flowers, wine, or anything connected to love.

PINK CANDLES
(ANY SIZE)

ROSE PETALS

ROSE ESSENTIAL OIL

HIMALAYAN SALT

1 Set up your bathroom in a way that you find relaxing and romantic.

2 Light some pink candles and enjoy the nice atmosphere they create.

3 Think of your bathroom as a cauldron. Fill it up with warm water and add all your magickal ingredients. Think about how you'd like to appear and how you'd like to love yourself.

4 Recite this magickal chant:

> "GLAMOUR WITHIN,
>
> GLAMOUR WITHOUT,
>
> I'M LOVED AND BEAUTIFUL,
>
> WITH NO DOUBT!"

5 Enjoy your bath. When you feel your skin has absorbed all the magickal energies, the spell can be considered done.

GUARDIAN SPELL

Our house is our safe place, and that's why we want it to be protected from negative feelings. This spell will create a guardian that will send all bad energies away. The perfect plant for this spell is a cactus. If you can't find one, any plant from the desert will do—even better if it has spikes.

A CACTUS

COFFEE GROUNDS

EGGSHELLS

BEER

1   Create the guardian food to feed your cactus. Mix together the eggshells, the coffee grounds, and a small splash of beer.

2   While you incorporate the food into the soil, say:

"I NOW CHARGE YOU WITH THE
PROTECTION OF THIS HOME,

AND ALL WITHIN IT.

I TRUST THE ENERGY OF THIS SPELL,

I TRUST YOU BELONG TO ME.
AND I BELONG TO YOU.

BE BLESSED IN THE DAYLIGHT,

BE BLESSED IN THE DARK NIGHT,

WE SHALL BE FRIENDS.

SO MOTE IT BE!"

3   Place your cactus near your front door.

CHARM TO ATTRACT A NEW LOVE

When we are balanced, loved by our friends, and feeling stable, we might feel ready for a new love. Perform this spell to open the doors to a new romantic relationship.

A PINK OR RED CLOTH

ACACIA, LAVENDER, ROSE, JASMINE, AND MYRTLE FLOWER PETALS

A COPPER COIN OR RING YOU DON'T WEAR OFTEN

A RED FELT HEART

A BLUE RIBBON

SALT

WATER

A CANDLE (LIT)

1 Fill your cloth with the flower petals, your coin or ring, and the red heart.

2 Tie the cloth with the blue ribbon, forming seven knots.

3 Cast a circle and call the four elements.

4 Breathe on it to symbolize air, pass it over the candle's flame to symbolize fire, sprinkle it with water (to symbolize water), and then tip it into salt to symbolize earth.

5 Hold it and charge it with your personal energy. Once you've done that, you've created your charm.

PROSPERITY SPELL

This spell will help you attract more money into

your life, with the help of the moon's energies. You might receive unexpected money or find a new job as a result of this spell.

A FULL MOON   A SILVER COIN

1   Place the coin in a position where the light of the moon reflects off of it.

2   Say:

"LOVELY MOON,

BRING ME YOUR ABUNDANCE,

BRING ME YOUR WEALTH,

FILL MY HANDS FULL OF SILVER AND GOLD,

MY DESIRE IS NOW TOLD!"

3   Repeat it three times.

4   Bury the coin underground for the entire night. (If you don't have a garden, leave it under the Full Moon.)

5   In the morning, dig up the coin and then put it in your wallet. The spell will work until the next Full Moon.

CALL ME SPELL

This spell is performed when you want someone to call you. The person in your mind might call you five minutes, five hours, or five days after the spell.

PARCHMENT   A NEEDLE

A PEN   A PHONE

1 Twice, write down the name of the person who has to call you, creating a circle shape—the two ends have to meet.

2 While you meditate on the spell, jab a needle in the middle of the circle.

3 Place the parchment under your phone.

4 You boost the power by saying:

"BY THIS PENTAGRAM I WEAR,

FOUR ELEMENTS: WATER, FIRE, EARTH AND AIR,

RULED BY SPIRITS AS ALL SHOULD BE

AS I SPEAK,

SO MOTE IT BE!"

(If you decide to read these lines, it would help if you were wearing a Pentagram.)

WISHING SPELL

This spell is performed when you'd like a wish to come true. To receive from the universe what you desire, it is important to practice kindness: you can receive only if you give. Use this spell as inspiration to practice more kindness.

DIFFERENT-COLORED
CANDLES

A WHITE CANDLE

A BOWL

SOME COINS

1   Drip some colored wax on the bottom of the bowl,
    then stick the white candle in the warm wax. The
    different colors represent your different needs.

2   Every morning, light the candle and leave a coin in
    the bowl.

3   Make your wish for the day and blow out the candle
    before leaving your house.

4   When the bowl is full of coins, you can take most
    of them back. Leave a few to remain as seeds. Use
    the few coins left for random acts of kindness: help
    homeless people or buy a treat for the neighbor's
    kid. Your generosity will return threefold, keeping
    the magick of benevolence, the mundane, and the
    divine alive.

REPAIR A FRIENDSHIP SPELL

In the course of a friendship, we might accidentally
hurt each other. It is okay to make mistakes sometimes. If a friendship becomes complicated, this
spell will help you find the solution.

LAVENDER SHOWER
GEL

PARCHMENT

PINK PEN

A SUNFLOWER OR AN
OBJECT WITH THE
SAME SHAPE

A PINK CANDLE

1   Take a warm shower using the lavender gel, and imagine all the bad feelings going away.

2   Light the candle, close a magick circle, and invoke the deity Kuan Yin by saying:

> "KUAN YIN, GODDESS OF PEACEFUL RELATIONSHIPS,
>
> I ASK YOU TO ASSIST ME TONIGHT IN THE ACT OF REPAIRING MY FRIENDSHIP WITH [THE NAME OF YOUR FRIEND].
>
> I PRAY THEE, HELP ME TO BRING THE FRIENDSHIP BACK!"

3   Meditate on the good things about the relationship you have with your friend. When your heart is filled with love, use a pink pen to write down your feelings and read them aloud while holding the sunflower.

4   Repeat:

> "KUAN YIN, GODDESS OF PEACEFUL RELATIONSHIPS,
>
> INSTILL IN THIS SUNFLOWER YOUR PACIFIC ENERGIES!"

5   Put the sunflower on the paper. Then thank the deity by saying:

> "KUAN YIN, GODDESS OF PEACEFUL RELATIONSHIPS,

I AM SO GRATEFUL FOR ANYTHING YOU
WILL DECIDE TO GIVE ME. STAY IF YOU WANT,
GO IF YOU HAVE TO. I DISMISS YOU NOW.

BLESSED BE!"

6   Open the circle, let the candle burn, and give the
     sunflower to your friend.

CONCLUSION

It is my hope that this book inspired you to start your magickal journey. Whether you're new to Witchcraft or an experienced practitioner, may this book be helpful when you need it.

Magick is an incredible practice that connects us with our beautiful planet and fulfills our hearts. Nature is what gives us life and happiness—it nourishes our bodies and souls. Deciding to work with nature is an enormous act of kindness we gift to ourselves and those around us.

Remember that your magickal path is yours alone; there are no rules that you have to follow or mistakes that can end your journey. Be kind and patient with yourself, allow yourself to make mistakes, and learn along the way.

I am very grateful for the time you've spent reading this book. I wish you a life full of magick and happiness.

BLESSED BE!

ISABELLA FERRARI was born and raised in Italy. After living for more than two years at ILTK, the acclaimed Buddhist institute, she became a meditation teacher. She then lived in London for a few years to explore her interest in music and art. She is the author of the novel *Ocean Crayon*, and wrote for her own website and many important magazines as a music journalist. Her passion for spirituality and religions inspired her to deeply study the different branches of Witchcraft and Paganism and create her project Greenwitchcom. Find her on Instagram @greenwitchcom.

ABOUT CIDER MILL PRESS BOOK PUBLISHERS

Good ideas ripen with time. From seed to harvest, Cider Mill Press brings fine reading, information, and entertainment together between the covers of its creatively crafted books. Our Cider Mill bears fruit twice a year, publishing a new crop of titles each spring and fall.

"Where Good Books Are Ready for Press"

Visit us online at
cidermillpress.com

or write to us at
PO Box 454
12 Spring St.
Kennebunkport, Maine 04046